Diving & Snorkeling

Australia's
Great Barrier Reef

Len Zell

LONELY PLANET PUBLICATIONS
Melbourne • Oakland • London • Paris

Diving & Snorkeling Australia's Great Barrier Reef
- A Lonely Planet Pisces Book

1st edition
November, 1999

Published by
Lonely Planet Publications
192 Burwood Road, Hawthorn, Victoria 3122, Australia

Other offices
150 Linden Street, Oakland, California 94607, USA
10A Spring Place, London NW5 3BH, UK
1 rue du Dahomey, 75011 Paris, France

Photographs
by photographers as indicated

Front cover photograph
A diver explores soft corals on the *Yongala*,
by Andy Skimming

Back cover photographs
Masked boobies on Flinder's Reef, by Len Zell
Diver with anemone, by Michael Aw
Aerial view of Heron Island, by Michael Aw

Some of the images in this guide are available for
licensing from **Lonely Planet Images**
email: lpi@lonelyplanet.com.au

ISBN 0 86442 763 8

text & maps © Lonely Planet 1999
photographs © photographers as indicated 1999
dive site maps are Transverse Mercator projection

Printed by H&Y Printing Ltd., Hong Kong

Contents

Author

Len Zell

Len is a biologist with 25 years of diving, research, marine park and education experience on the Great Barrier Reef. He is an active underwater stills photographer who has recently discovered video. He is a respected reef guide who has consulted on films, books and documentaries.

Len chaired Dive Queensland Inc., and has led courses in marine biology, reef ecology and underwater photography. He spent six one-month seasons diving with the Queensland Museum, exploring the remains of the HMS *Pandora*. He has worked for the Great Barrier Reef Marine Park Authority and Queensland Marine Parks. In recognition of his work at the Australian Institute of Marine Science, a coral—*Australogyra zelli*—was named after him.

Len's extensive diving experience is enhanced by his travels in the South Pacific, from Hawaii to Easter Island via Polynesia and Cook Islands, Fiji, Tonga, Niue, Wallis and Futuna as well as Lord Howe Island, Papua New Guinea, Florida, Thailand, Tahiti, Red Sea and Grand Cayman Island.

Len uses primarily Nikonos cameras with Kodachrome 64 and Fuji Velvia film and Olympus systems for above water. He now lives and sells real estate in Port Douglas and can be contacted on email: lenzell@portdouglas.tnq.com.au

From the Author

This guide would have been impossible without the input of a wonderful group of divers and reefies. I want to thank specifically Isobel Bennett for her insights into reefs, Roslyn Bullas and Deb Miller for Lonely Planet support, Wendy Morris and Peter Gesner for writing, editorial, in-water and general support, John Barnett for photos, and John Morris, Marillyn Morris and Charlie Veron for their enthusiasm for the reefs. Also thanks to Andy Skimming for his help with photos and rediscovering those little critters in the seagrasses of Watson's Bay.

This book was only possible with contributions from the following individuals, who helped broaden my perspective for each site. Thanks to: Mike Ball, Stan Kielbaskas, Craig, Rich Davies—Mike Ball Dive Expeditions; Adam Masterton, Ron Whitney—Lady Elliot Island Resort; Scott Gilbert—Lady Musgrave Cruises; Ian Gray—P&O Resorts; Allan Marsters, Birgit Kellermann, Robert Freitag—Capricorn Diving; Sarah Grant—Ocean Rafting; Nikki Dyer, Elmer Tenharken—Fantasea; Jeannie Kraak and team—Reef Dive; Mark Mayer (Sharkey); Danny Dwyer, Cam Froude, Keith Payne—Oceania Dive; Denis McDowall—Coral Princess Cruises; Melanie Abela—Pure Pleasure Cruises; Fraser Bruce—Cairns Dive Center; Ian Stevens—Sunlover Cruises; John Weisgerber—Pro Dive; Jon Burnett—Seahorse Sail/Dive; Peter Davon—Tusa Dive; Greg Brooker—Sea Star II; Alan Wallish, Verushka Matchett—Passions of Paradise; Phil Woodhead—Rum Runner; Kai Steinbeck—Deep Dea Diver's Den; Iain Ralston—Haba Dive; Colin Coxon—Quicksilver; Chris Upite—Big Mama; Mark Westwater—Taka II Dive Adventures; John Rumney, Andy Dunstan—Undersea Explorer; Peter Montgomery—Lizard Island Lodge; Richard Webb, Paula Wallace—Big Cat Green Island; Darren Newton—Salty's Dive Centre; Cathie Fahey—Diver's Mecca; Rick and Mel Wakefield—Downrite Adventures; GBRMPA and Q.DOE and Environment Australia. Also thanks to all those many wonderful people who provided additional help and information.

Contributing Photographers

Many thanks to all the talented photographers who contributed colorful images to help illustrate this book. They include: Michael Aw, John Barnett, Bob Charlton, Michael Collins, Philippe Guiquel, Bob Halstead, John Hay, Craig Lamotte, Michael McKay, Paul Sinclair, Andy Skimming, Phil Woodhead, Len Zell and Neville Zell.

From the Publisher

This first edition was published in Lonely Planet's U.S. office under the guidance of Roslyn Bullas, Pisces publishing manager. In the coral-encrusted fish tank Debra Miller swam through subjects and verbs, editing the text and photos while Emily Douglas designed the book and cover with flare and finesse. Patrick Bock navigated the cartographic ship through the many cays, reefs and islands by creating excellent maps, with helpful dispatches from lighthouse keeper/U.S. Cartography Manager Alex Guilbert. Roisin O'Dwyer also assisted with maps. Portions of the text were adapted from Lonely Planet's *Islands of Australia's Great Barrier Reef* and *Queensland*. Many thanks to Wendy Smith for donning her proofreader's mask, Kevin Anglin for helping with depth gauge conversions, and Hayden Foell for his illustrative prowess. Also a whale of a thanks to Bill Alevizon, who checked the marine life section for scientific accuracy.

A friendly "cheers mate" to Rich, Kate and Brett for their sleuthing services in finding "The Frenchman" and to Bob Halstead and the folks at LPI for some last-minute photo help. A special thanks and hats off to Len Zell, whose grace, expertise and passion for the GBR are reflected in the pages of this book.

Lonely Planet Pisces Books

Lonely Planet acquired the Pisces line of diving and snorkeling books in 1997. The series is being developed and substantially revamped over the next few years. We welcome your comments and suggestions.

Pisces Pre-Dive Safety Guidelines

Before embarking on a scuba diving, skin diving or snorkeling trip, carefully consider the following to help ensure a safe and enjoyable experience:

- Possess a current diving certification card from a recognized scuba diving instructional agency (if scuba diving)
- Be sure you are healthy and feel comfortable diving
- Obtain reliable information about physical and environmental conditions at the dive site (e.g., from a reputable local dive operation)
- Be aware of local laws, regulations and etiquette about marine life and environment
- Dive at sites within your experience level; if possible, engage the services of a competent, professionally trained dive instructor or divemaster

Underwater conditions vary significantly from one region, or even site, to another. Seasonal changes can significantly alter any site and dive conditions. These differences influence the way divers dress for a dive and what diving techniques they use.

There are special requirements for diving in any area, regardless of location. Before your dive, ask about the environmental characteristics that can affect your diving and how trained local divers deal with these considerations.

Warning & Request

Things change—dive site conditions, regulations, topside information. Nothing stays the same for long. Your feedback on this book will be used to help update and improve the next edition more useful. Excerpts from your correspondence may appear in *Planet Talk*, our quarterly newsletter, or *Comet*, our monthly email newsletter. Please let us know if you do not want your letter published or your name acknowledged.

Correspondence can be addressed to:
Lonely Planet Publications
Pisces Books
150 Linden Street
Oakland, CA 94607
email: pisces@lonelyplanet.com

Introduction

Australia, the island continent, is one of the most desirable tourist destinations in the world, yet many American and European travelers are daunted by the long haul of jet travel it takes to get to this wonderfully unique and friendly country. Those who make the trip find the effort well worth it. Sophisticated, modern cities and remote country towns line scorching deserts and winter snowfields. The extreme climate supports mining, vineyards,

PHILIPPE GUIQUEL

crops of all varieties, a profusion of wildlife and a unique human history woven out of isolation and multiculturalism. All this and some of the best, most accessible diving found anywhere in the world.

Australia has superb diving around its entire coast and in several inland cave systems, but the big draw is the barrier reef—the world's largest. Bigger than Britain, almost the size of Texas (but a lot deeper!) and stretching 2,300km (1,400 miles) from north to south, the Great Barrier Reef (GBR) is enormous. This book concentrates on the GBR Province, encompassing an area of over 1 million sq km (386,000 sq miles)—including the whole GBR, nearby Coral Sea reefs (under

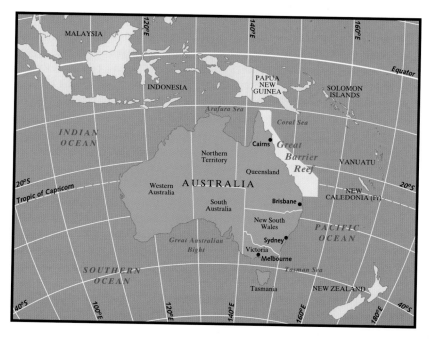

Australian jurisdiction) and the Torres Strait (under joint jurisdiction with Papua New Guinea).

The GBR is alive with about 400 species of coral, 2,000 species of fish, 4,000 molluscs and countless other invertebrates. Six of the world's seven species of sea turtles breed here, and the diversity doesn't stop there. GBR coastal, reef and water habitats support a myriad of single-celled organisms that free-float in the nutrient-rich waters, in the sand grains, mud flats, and seagrass beds and among the reefs and rocks, playing an important role in the food chain.

The islands of the GBR can be small bare "deserts" swept away with each major storm or they can be covered in lush rainforest or mangrove. Some are home to nesting seabirds and a vast array of wildlife. Between the reefs and islands are shoal areas of coral and algae (bioherms), with incredible bottom-dwelling animals living on the mud, sand and shell bottoms.

With a huge variety of habitats stretching across the continental shelf, the potential for diving, snorkeling and scientific discovery is immeasurable. Anyone lucky enough to have dived thousands of times on the GBR still has only a general glimpse of the whole system. Cyclones, storms, bleaching events, coral growth and crown-of-thorns sea star invasions combine with time and the passing of seasons to continually change the appearance of each reef.

Many people describe the GBR as having the best diving in the world—it has the potential for that title simply because of its size and accessibility, habitat and species diversity. Keep in mind, however, that you will not necessarily experience "brochure weather"—when clear sunny days, calm seas and beautiful people all come together. To really discover the GBR, you need to be willing to experience it in all weather, areas and seasons. Stick by the old sayings, "The

LEN ZELL
Noddy and crested terns nest on GBR cays.

best diving is in the water" and, "A bad day's diving is better than a good day's work," and the GBR will not let you down.

The world's single largest living system, the GBR is part of the superb Indo-Pacific coral reef system, extending from the Red Sea to Easter Island. In this book, accessible sites are described to enhance your understanding and enjoyment of the GBR's unique ecosystem. You'll also get a brief overview of the primary accessible Coral Sea reefs.

For organizational purposes, the dive sites are divvied up into nine regions and their surrounding areas, starting with the Capricorn & Bunker Groups in the south, going north to the Swain Reefs, Pompey Complex, Whitsunday Islands, Townsville & Magnetic Island, Cairns, Port Douglas, Far Northern Reefs, and ending with the Torres Strait in the north.

You'll get specific information on each dive site, including the behavioral patterns of the marine life you can expect to see, informative notes on reef formations, depth and recommended diving expertise. Get historical insight on some of GBR's most famous shipwrecks (the barrier reef has tortured navigators for centuries!) and when it's finally time to dry off, turn to the Practicalities and Activities & Attractions sections for helpful topside information.

PHIL WOODHEAD

A diver explores an open-topped cave at Holmes Reef.

Overview

The GBR waters extend from Lady Elliot Island in the south near Bundaberg north to Bramble Cay and Black Rock in the Torres Strait almost to Papua New Guinea. The GBR should really be named the "Great Barrier of Reefs" as about 3,000 individual reefs—and some 900 islands—are scattered along the Queensland Continental Shelf an average depth of 40m (130ft).

The shelf is from as little as 23km- (14 miles-) wide, from Cape Melville to Tydeman Reef, up to 270km- (168 miles-) wide, from Cape Clinton—north of Gladstone and Yeppon—to Elusive Reef on the eastern side of the Swain Reefs. This outer edge of the GBR and the continental shelf is fringed by the Queensland Trench, which is up to 2,000m (6,600ft) deep.

East of the Queensland Trench, the flat-topped Coral Sea plateaus give rise to the Coral Sea reefs and atolls. Note that there are atolls in the Coral Sea, but none within the GBR waters. About a third of GBR reefs are fringing reefs—reefs dotted along the mainland coast and around most of the islands—with the other two-thirds scattered all over the continental shelf.

A videographer shoots spiky soft coral on a northern reef.

Atolls, Cays or Islands—What's the Diff?

Coral Sea Atolls Unlike true coral atolls—ring-like coral islands that nearly or entirely enclose a lagoon—the outer Coral Sea reefs are primarily a series of reefs surrounding a lagoon on a submerged mountain top or similar plateau. The inner Coral Sea reefs to the north and south are more like true atolls.

Continental or Mainland Islands These islands are remnants of the mainland, protruding above the sea from the continental shelf. Usually volcanic or sedimentary in origin, they support quite different animals and vegetation than cays. The reefs around these islands are there as a result of the island—the reefs having grown out from the island.

Coral Cays Pronounced both "kays" and "keys," cays are formed by debris piled up from the reef edges and tops. This debris is composed mainly of dead coral, shells, calcareous algae and little single-celled animals called forams. Cays range from pure soft "coral" sands to those of shingle, rubble and boulders. Some cays, such as the Turtle Islands in the north, are remnants of old uplifted fossil reefs.

Rainforest, grassy, herbaceous and mangrove plant communities grow on GBR cays. Many are important bird and turtle nesting or roosting areas. They support differing plant communities due to the their rainfall and isolated locations. Green, Heron and Lady Elliot Islands are all coral cays. The mangrove cays at Low and Hope Isles and other reefs to the north are primarily shingle and rubble perched on top of coral reefs. Snorkeling in the mangroves is amazing. Corals and shells grow on mangrove roots, while horseshoe clams, mini coral heads, seagrasses and upside-down sea jellies join the masses of fish—a far cry from the general belief that mangroves are muddy, smelly places.

A rainbow stretches over Herald Cay.

The Coral Sea is classified here to include the reefs and islands outside the 500m (1,640ft) depth contour of the GBR. This area is part of the Pacific Ocean and it and the Coral Sea extend into the Queensland coast. Dive Queensland operators agreed that the "Coral Sea Dive Sites" would be defined as only those outside the GBR boundary. Included are a series of atolls and associated islands within Australian territorial waters. Coral Sea reefs covered in this book include, from the south, Flinders Reefs, Holmes Reefs, Bougainville Reef and Osprey Reef.

The GBR is intimately linked, by ocean waters and currents, to all other reefs of the Indian and Pacific Oceans. Most species found in the Red Sea, Hawaii and southeast Pacific are the same as, or similar to, species found on the GBR. Alternately, very few GBR species occur in the Caribbean Sea or Atlantic Oceans.

History

During the ice ages, at least 40,000 years ago and before, the Australian Aboriginals first made their way across land bridges from Southeast Asia. They were probably mainly coastal dwellers and would have lived at the edge of today's continental shelf, on areas 150m (490ft) below today's sea surface. As the ice melted and the sea level rose, the Aboriginal people moved across the submerging coastal plain. Their journey took them away from the old shelf-edge fringing reefs, past the disappearing fossil reefs, which would look like flat-topped limestone hills, until they were able to remain at the present coastal and island situations we see today.

More recent human history includes use of the northern areas up to 5,000 years ago by the Macassan people—a seafaring group with a now-traceable genetic presence in the coastal Aboriginal people.

The first recorded European visit to the (northern) GBR was probably by the Portuguese Manoel Gidinho de Eredia in 1601, although there is strong evidence that fellow Portuguese had come up to 50 years before. A Spaniard, Luis Vaez de Torres, passed through the Torres Strait in 1606, but it wasn't until 1770 that Captain James Cook made the first fully recorded "discovery" of the GBR. Cook even ran aground on it, which foreshadowed some of the problems it would later give navigators.

Many others followed. Two notable events include William Bligh's longboat trip through the area (after the *Bounty* mutiny) in 1789. The trip produced a quality chart of both Bligh's Passage and Restoration Island at Cape Weymouth to the north. The second notable event was the wreck of the *Pandora*, which ran aground and sank on the northern GBR in 1791, taking four of the 14 mutineers from the *Bounty* and 31 crew members with her. The ship's cat was on the topmast the morning after the sinking, but there is no record of it after that.

JOHN HAY

An Aboriginal, whose ancestors first came to Australia by now-submerged land bridges, spears a mud crab.

Matthew Flinders was another great navigator, explorer and scientist who circumnavigated Australia, charting it for the British Admiralty. In the early 1800s he charted much of the southern GBR shipping route, its coast and islands, and parts of the Coral Sea. He left the GBR through what is now known as Flinders Passage. Much of his work is still seen on charts today.

It wasn't until Lt. Charles Jeffreys on the brig *Kangaroo* bravely sailed and charted the inner route in 1815 that more sizable ships were able to take the calmer inside route along the GBR. Jeffreys was followed by fellow navigators Phillip Parker King in the *Mermaid* in 1819 and many others.

Surveys and charting continued in the 1840s and '50s. The advent of steamships and the completion of the Suez Canal in 1869 made the route around the north of Australia and inside the GBR a far faster and shorter voyage from Europe than the old route around the southern tip of Africa and the south of Australia.

With most of the routes now charted it was possible for more exploration and, inevitably, exploitation of the area to begin. Bêche-de-mer (sea cucumber), pearl, turbo and trochus shell harvesting combined with guano mining meant, in addition to passing ships, many smaller vessels were now plying the waters. Scores of ships of all sizes were wrecked during these times and many remain unfound.

Much of the older harvesting methods have been improved, with bêche-de-mer fishery continuing, and pearl and trochus harvesting still happening in the north. Today, modern trawlers sweep large areas of the sea floor and shelf between the reefs, trawling for prawns (shrimp), scallops and crayfish. There is a major push to stop this activity due to habitat destruction and wasted by-catch—often weighing up to 10 times more than the intended catch. A variety of small vessels fish for live trout, reef fish and the pelagic mackerel and tuna. By far the greatest use of the reef today is tourism and recreation, with thousands of people visiting the reefs daily.

With increased use of the GBR came the need for management. Through the late 1960s and early '70s consciousness about the detrimental effects of limestone mining, oil drilling, general degradation and reef overuse grew. Public concern prompted the establishment of the Great Barrier Reef Marine Park Authority (GBRMPA, known locally as "g-broom-pa") in 1975. Later, in 1981, the GBR won designation as a World Heritage Site by the United Nations Educational, Scientific and Cultural Organization (UNESCO). Today, the GBRMPA manages the waters around the GBR, while the Queensland National Parks & Wildlife (QNPW), an offshoot of the Environmental Protection Agency, manages the GBR "lands." Obviously, the land and water areas overlap, so there is much cooperation between these two organizations.

Note: The area within the so-named GBR Marine Park region is often used to describe the whole GBR, when it in fact leaves out the large area north of 10°41'—from Cape York to Papua New Guinea. When you see GBR statistics beware of this variance! This book refers to the entire GBR, including the northern section.

Geography

The GBR and Coral Sea seamounts were dry on and off over their reef growth, with the last series of ice ages beginning about 150,000 years ago. After the last ice age—which ended about 20,000 years ago—reefs began to resubmerge. Sea level stabilized at its present height about 6,000 to 8,000 years ago. Since then, a new veneer of coral has grown over the reefs' fossil remains, which date back to only 400,000 years.

Earlier estimates placed the origins of the system from 2 million years old in the south, to 12 million years in the north, due to the system's slow drift into the warm tropical waters. Depths of old reef growth vary from 1,500m (5,000ft) in the Gulf of Papua in the north, 250m (800ft) off Townsville (roughly the middle of the GBR) and 150m (500ft) near Heron Island in the south.

Not a lot of evidence of the ice ages can be seen in the fossil reefs below the latest growth. This lack of evidence is due to erosion that took place while the reefs were dry during the last ice age. This was when sea level dropped 150m (500ft) below its present level. The erosion is apparent in layers of land sedimentation over and between the superimposed reef surfaces. Old river beds are still seen in underwater sonar scanning and seismic profiling out to the edge of the continental shelf, between present-day reefs. Recent drilling has also found charcoal and mangrove mud below the reefs and underneath the overlaying fossil reefs. Reefs today expose only about a fifth of their total structure—the rest is hidden below the shelf mud, sand and other sediments that were washed there during the previous dry ice ages.

Differing rates of submergence and coastal and tidal affects have caused the great variation in reef structures today. Some are flat-topped plates of reef, while others are confused masses of little reefs gradually growing together on top of an old submerged reef surface—these are also reflections of the rising or sinking of the coastal edge of the Australian plate.

Archaeologists are constantly searching for submerged caves on the GBR that may indicate dry periods and, of greatest excitement, human presence. Divers were recently lucky enough to find some caves with such evidence on Tijou Reef (Mr. Walker's Caves), which may hold some clues to these dry periods.

LEN ZELL
Many of the GBR's coastal fringing reefs expose at low tide.

What is a Coral Reef?

The reefs of the GBR are actually a thin veneer of living coral, algae and other marine life on top of what could be described as the world's largest rubbish dump. As the corals grow, their symbiotic relationship with the single-celled algae in their tissues—zooxanthellae—produces several waste products. One of these wastes is calcium carbonate, or limestone. As the living layer of corals dump this limestone, each species uses a different stacking design for the crystals. This is what gives us the great and beautiful diversity of hard white coral skeletons.

Leeward Side   Windward Side

| Reef Back Bommies | Reef Flat | Coral Cay | Lagoon | Reef Flat | Reef Front |

Profile of a Typical Reef

As the colonies of coral die or are smashed by storms, killed by polluted, fresh, hot or cold waters, or eaten by parrotfish or crown-of-thorns sea stars, they leave their bleached skeleton behind. These skeletons make ideal settlements for many organisms that blend into the matrix of materials that form a reef—each reef is thus a jumble of bits and pieces.

Waves and currents are the major factors determining the shape of any reef. Reefs of the GBR tend to have a southeasterly face, which is hammered most of the year by the prevailing southeasterly winds. This leads to the smooth algal rim on the top edge. Spurs, grooves, channels and notches follow the slope down to many different structures determined by depth, location, wave action and currents. Coral and algal structures on the reef fronts tend to be solid and smooth. On the "back" of the reef we find fragile staghorn coral thickets, shallow plate corals, sand slopes and isolated coral heads (bommies). Occasionally a cyclone or severe storm will bring wind and waves from the north or northwest, which can devastate a back-reef edge in a matter of hours.

Reefs are like enormous ocean filters. With the high capture rate of nutrients and growth rate of corals and algae, coral reefs are highly productive systems. A reef is well-described as a "wall of mouths."

The speed with which corals and other organisms grow, are smothered, buried, broken or otherwise altered is mind-boggling. Different times of day, tides, years, El Niño, La Niña, crown-of-thorns invasions, bleaching events and coastal run-off all contribute to this constantly changing world. Just as the coral species and animals determine the shape of the skeleton, the force of the waves and wind determine the shape of the reef and its features.

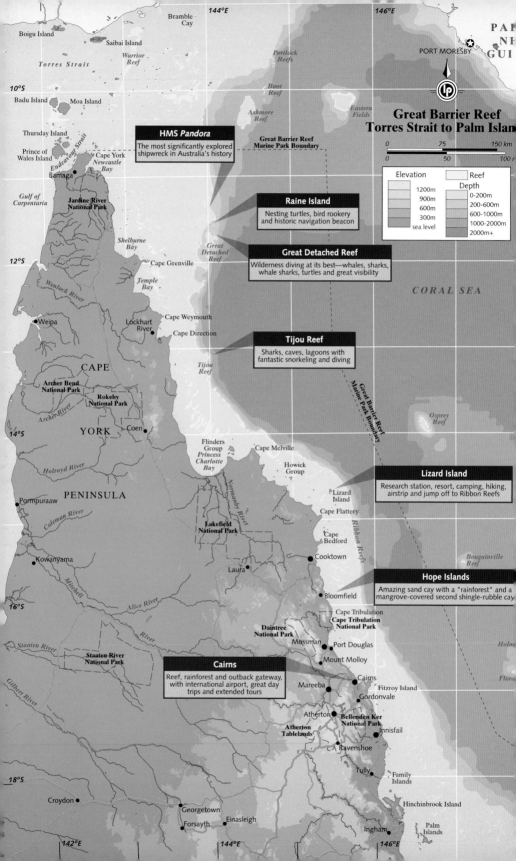

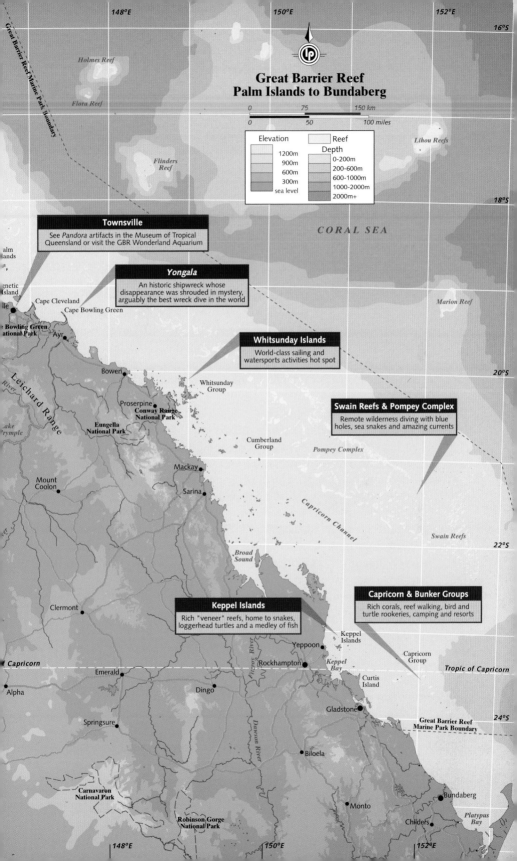

Great Barrier Reef
Palm Islands to Bundaberg

Elevation
- 1200m
- 900m
- 600m
- 300m
- sea level

Reef
Depth
- 0-200m
- 200-600m
- 600-1000m
- 1000-2000m
- 2000m+

Holmes Reef

Flora Reef

Flinders Reef

Lihou Reefs

CORAL SEA

Marion Reef

Great Barrier Reef Marine Park Boundary

Townsville
See *Pandora* artifacts in the Museum of Tropical Queensland or visit the GBR Wonderland Aquarium

Yongala
An historic shipwreck whose disappearance was shrouded in mystery, arguably the best wreck dive in the world

Whitsunday Islands
World-class sailing and watersports activities hot spot

Swain Reefs & Pompey Complex
Remote wilderness diving with blue holes, sea snakes and amazing currents

Keppel Islands
Rich "veneer" reefs, home to snakes, loggerhead turtles and a medley of fish

Capricorn & Bunker Groups
Rich corals, reef walking, bird and turtle rookeries, camping and resorts

alm lands

enetic Island

lle

Cape Cleveland

Cape Bowling Green

Bowling Green ational Park

Ayr

Bowen

Proserpine

Conway Range National Park

Eungella National Park

Whitsunday Group

Cumberland Group

Pompey Complex

Mackay

Sarina

Capricorn Channel

Mount Coolon

Leichard Range

ake rymple

Broad Sound

Swain Reefs

Clermont

Keppel Islands

Yeppoon

Rockhampton

Keppel Bay

Capricorn Group

Capricorn

Emerald

Dingo

Curtis Island

Tropic of Capricorn

Alpha

Gladstone

Springsure

Great Barrier Reef Marine Park Boundary

Biloela

Carnavaron National Park

Robinson Gorge National Park

Bundaberg

Monto

Childers

Platypus Bay

148°E   150°E   152°E

16°S

18°S

20°S

22°S

24°S

LEN ZELL

Practicalities

Climate

Weather on the GBR is said, by the locals, to be predictably unpredictable—always expect the unexpected. Being in the southern hemisphere, GBR seasons are the reverse of those in Europe and the U.S.—summer is December to March and winter is June to September.

Because of the GBR's length, which stretches between 9 and 25°S (the same distance as New York to Miami, or the same latitudes and distance as Miami to Trinidad), there is a significant difference in the weather from north to south. The whole complex is in the tropics, except for Heron Island and the Bunker Group, which straddle the Tropic of Capricorn, so anything below is considered "sub-tropical." Distance from the coast and sea state have a significant influence on weather as well.

Summer northwest monsoons—seldom extending south of Mackay—give the north a distinct wet season from December to March. It is usually hotter and wetter in the north, and Australia's highest rainfall area is on the coast at Tully, just south of Cairns. Humidity during the wet season can be oppressive for short periods, but at sea on a boat or an island allows you escape from the less comfortable weather on the mainland. July to September are drier. Temperatures are cooler in the south—getting down to 14°C (57°F) on Lady Elliot Island—and significantly colder on the mainland, where the four seasons are more distinct.

Winds vary from long periods of calm—usually October to February—to cyclonic (hurricane) conditions, which can occur from December to April. There is a good cyclone warning system so don't worry about being caught out. The benefits of diving at this time of the year far outweigh the disadvantages—if there is a cyclone around and you aren't too close you'll usually have superb calm weather. The prevailing southeasterlies blow from about April to October but can occur any time. Fortunately, most reefs offer a protected side regardless of wind direction.

The water temperature tends to lag behind the air temperature about one to two months as you go south. Water is warm all year round in the north, from about 24 to 30°C (75 to 86°F). As you go south it gradually gets cooler, dropping to 20°C (68°F) in summer and up to 28°C (82°F) in winter.

GBR waters are well-mixed so there is usually no distinct thermocline (temperature change) as you go deeper. Thermoclines still occur on hot still days with minimal tide changes or where the colder oceanic waters slop up onto the continental shelf, beneath the warmer shelf waters.

Tide Talk

The gravitational pull of the moon and position of the Earth in relation to the sun drive tides so they change throughout the month and year. When the sun and moon are in line we get **spring tides**, and when they are at right angles to each other we get **neap tides**. Accurate tide tables are available for most of the GBR, but turn to the locals for subtle regional variations.

Divers like to plan their diving around neap tides to ensure maximum visibility and lower tide flow. Spring tides bring dirtier water, stronger currents and often worse weather. The GBR generally has tidal changes twice daily—two highs and two lows. At Thursday Island, tides are almost once daily due to the connection, through the Torres Strait, between the Coral and Arafura seas.

At the southern end of the reef and at Townsville, the maximum change is about 3m (10ft). As you move toward Broad Sound (between Mackay and Rockhampton), the ranges increase and usually decrease as you move away from the coast. Outside of Broad Sound it is not uncommon to get currents of up to 15km/h (9mph). Local dive operators know how to avoid the channels, so listen to the briefings.

Tidal currents are a great reason to always dive with a safety sausage or other signalling device. Learn how to recognize good safety holds on the bottom, plan your dives, have good surface backup and you'll be set for some great drift dives.

Brochure photographs never reflect the true variability of the GBR's visibility. In coastal areas, it is common to have 1 to 3m (3 to 10ft) visibility and then just a few kilometers offshore it can jump to 8 to 15m (26 to 50ft) and to 20 to 35m (66 to 115ft) on the outer edge. In the Coral Sea, 50m (164ft) visibility is not uncommon.

Divers prepare for a night dive on Lady Musgrave Island.

Getting There

Australia is well-serviced with international flights coming into Sydney, Brisbane, Cairns, Darwin and Perth. Search around for the best flights that suit your itinerary and never ask anyone what they paid for their fare—it will always be less than yours! If you are on a dive trip only, try, if you can, to come directly into Cairns to avoid the delays of Sydney or Brisbane. If not, the state of Queensland has many coastal centers that serve as jumping off points to the GBR and Coral Sea.

Brisbane and Cairns are the international ports with regular domestic services to all the GBR points. Ansett and Qantas (Australia's two major domestic airlines) will book and supply services to all ports, either on their own flights or through a subsidiary. Lady Elliot, Brampton, Hamilton, Dunk and Lizard islands all have their own airstrips as do many of the Torres Strait Islands, with feeder airports at Bundaberg, Gladstone, Mackay, Proserpine, Townsville, Cairns and Thursday (Horn) Island. Iron Range has an airstrip, which is often used as a change-over point for far north expedition trips through Portland Roads, serviced from either Cairns or Thursday Island.

Gateway City - Cairns

With a population of 106,600, Cairns is now firmly established as one of Australia's top travel destinations and is the main jump-off port to GBR and Coral Sea destinations.

Not long ago, Cairns was a laid-back country town. Today, it's a modern, vivacious city that lives and breathes tourism. Cairns' airport is becoming one of the busiest in Australia and the flow of international arrivals continues to swell.

Many divers start or finish their GBR trip in Cairns and, although the city itself does not have a beach, dozens of operators run daily and hourly trips to offshore islands and reefs. Cairns is also the center for a host of other activities including white-water rafting, rainforest excursions, canoeing and, for adrenaline junkies, there's always bungee jumping or skydiving.

Getting Around

Regular bus services are available in most major centers—check with the local tourist or information center for fares and schedules. Taxis are everywhere, but can get expensive if you have a lot of running around to do before your dive trip. Renting a car is a good option if you have a group of people, are used to long road trips and have the time. Plan carefully, as the distances between cities are deceptively long. Rental cars are available at every center and airport. Some long-stay visitors even buy a car for the duration of their visit.

Coaches (most with movies) operate regularly between all centers and are the backpacker and budget traveler's choice of transportation. The buses are met by backpacker representatives at most major towns. You can take a train from

Brisbane to Cairns—an inexpensive and great way to see the countryside if you have the time. Hitchhiking is illegal. Boating between Townsville and Cairns, or Cairns and Cooktown is a great travel option, although diving is a lower priority than cruising, snorkeling and island visits.

Many of the dive operators offer a pick-up service from local accommodations to dive sites. Helicopters, floatplanes and amphibians can also take you directly to islands, boats or reef pontoons. Most are on a charter basis but some have regular services so check with the agents.

Entry

To visit Australia you need a current passport, valid for three months after your departure. Check with your local Australian consulate for visa requirements during your intended visit as it varies for length of stay and nature of your visit. Visas are free for three months and A$35 for six months. New Zealanders are exempt. You have to pay a departure tax when leaving Australia (usually included in your airfare).

To dive in Queensland you will be asked for your C-card and log book and often an operator will want to chat about what diving you have done. You will often be asked to sign a waiver form to protect the operator. If you wish to undertake a resort or introductory dive you are required to complete a medical questionnaire.

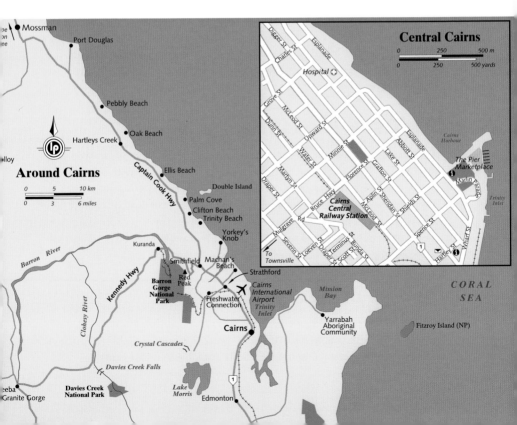

Money

Australia uses Australian dollars and cents only. Most other currencies are only acceptable at banks. Traveler's checks can be used but usually get a poorer rate at retail outlets. The use of credit cards is easy and widespread. There are many "hole in the wall" automatic teller machines (ATMs) and EFTPOS (Electronic Funds Transfer at Point Of Sale) outlets, which will work with most overseas accounts. Most dive services and accommodations accept credit cards.

Time

Australian Eastern Standard Time (GBR time) is 10 hours ahead of GMT except Heron Island Resort, which is 11 hours ahead. Queensland does not observe Daylight Saving's Time. When it's noon on the barrier reef, it's 11am in Tokyo, 2am in London and 6pm the day before in San Francisco. To find overseas times while in Australia, look at a local telephone directory under "International Codes," which lists all countries and their times relative to Australian time zones.

Electricity

Three-pin flat-point plugs are standard in Australia, although they differ from British three-point plugs. All electricity is on a 240V, 50Hz cycle, available on all resorts and overnight vessels although, as most are on a generator system, fluctuations are common so be careful with sensitive gear. Check beforehand if you need 110V, as it is rarely available. If you need multiple outlets, bring along a multi-plug "power board," converter plugs and a transformer. Most duty-free, hardware and luggage stores have converter plugs. Under no circumstances should you plug a non-240V unit into any Australian outlet.

Weights & Measures

Australia now follows the metric system, although many people (pre-1966!) still function on and understand imperial systems. In this book, both imperial and metric measurements are given, except for specific references to depth, which are given in meters only. Be careful to plan and undertake your dives in whatever system your gauges use. Divemasters are almost always capable of handling both measurements, but it's good to know what you're using before you head out. Also check out the conversion chart provided in the back of this book.

What to Bring

Topside: Prescription medicines, lenses and any other hard-to-get items should come with you. Many drugs sold overseas are not available in Australia. Otherwise most personal items are readily available in major centers.

Aussie Dive Lingo

In addition to the cheery "G'day" and a friendly "How ya goin mate?", you'll hear a variety of distinctly Aussie words, even in the universal language of diving. Here are just a few:

barra	barramundi
body condom	wetsuit
bommie	an isolated coral head
bugs	shovel-nosed lobster
cobia	kingfish
groper	grouper
hot boat	a drop-off dive boat that doesn't anchor or moor; divers do a parachute entry (see below)
men in grey suits	sharks
rubber duck	inflatable boat
parachute entry	when divers line up and follow each other into the water, like parachutists out of an aircraft. Done from a hot boat.
port	suitcase (short for "portmanteau")
stubby	bottle of beer
tinnie	can of beer
togs	swimsuit
torch	flashlight
wobby	wobbegong shark

It gets cold and windy at sea or on the islands so a good waterproof windbreaker or spray jacket is useful. A woolen sweater is advisable during winter in the south. A hat, sunglasses, sunscreen and a long-sleeved shirt for sun and burn protection are also important—there are reasons for the famous Aussie hats! Bug repellent is useful on the coast.

Dive-Related Equipment: For long periods of diving, you'll find a light wetsuit (3mm) is only suitable throughout the north. In the south, in winter to early summer, you'll want a 5mm full wetsuit, hood and boots. A lycra skin is ideal for snorkeling and sun protection.

Most operators rent out equipment at prices similar to most international destinations. Wetsuits are usually in good order. With competition and the high standards required by Queensland law, most operators now carry only well-serviced gear and offer computers in the rental package. As each operator is different, check beforehand (in writing if possible) to ensure you are getting the gear you want.

Queensland law says that each diver must dive with a buddy, wear a BC with a whistle, have an alternate air source, gauges, a protection suit, weights with quick release catch and, ideally, a computer. The law says divers should follow the DCIEM (Defence & Civil Institute of Environmental Medicine) tables and follow the instructions of the divemaster—in other words, the basic principles of safe diving are enshrined here in law. Be patient with the dive staff, as the precautions are for your safety and protection.

Repairs are readily available at coastal centers but generally not on boats or at resorts. Most locations sell all dive equipment, books and videos. Purchasing spare parts here can be risky, as most retail centers cater to a limited range of brands. Batteries are available almost everywhere.

Business Hours

Almost everything is open from 9am to 5pm weekdays, except for banks, which are open to 4pm and 5pm only on Fridays. Most shops open 9am to noon on Saturdays, with major shopping centers open all day Saturday and some on Sunday. For specialty items, it's best to shop before the weekend, when many specialty shops are closed.

Accommodations

Stay in a deluxe all-inclusive resort or pitch your tent on a remote reef—accommodations on the GBR coast run the gamut. Luxury 4- and 5-star accommodations are available in all major cities. Lady Elliot, Heron and Green islands have resorts and are coral cays. Many Whitsundays, along with Keppel, Magnetic, Orpheus, Fitzroy and Lizard islands are "mainland" islands and also have resorts.

Motels, hotels, caravan parks, camping areas and backpackers (privately run budget hostels) are available at all centers and many places in between. Most dive operators will be happy to suggest affiliated accommodations or a hotel that has the best deal for your requirements. Keep in mind that June and July are peak months; prices can really vary depending on when you go. Some islands (Great Keppel, Magnetic, Hook and Fitzroy) have hostels or other forms of budget accommodations.

Loading up the dive boat at the Lady Elliot Island Resort.

Dining & Food

Port Douglas is reputed to have the best dining available on the GBR coast, with a good range of restaurants at Cairns, Townsville and the Whitsundays areas. Popular seafood dishes include barramundi (found in rivers and estuaries in Northern Australia), coral trout, tuna, sweetlips, bream and mangrove jack. Fresh prawns are also popular. Excellent Australian wines are available, as are local beers—VB and XXXX ("four ex") are particular favorites after a hot day on the reef. For dessert try the pavlova—an "Australian" dessert made of meringue, whipped cream and fruit.

Things to Buy

Australia is a signatory to the CITES (Convention on International Trade in Endangered Species) Convention so it is illegal to trade in turtle shell, dugong, many shells, coral, black coral and the like. Treat your time on the reef as a "national park" experience and limit yourself to souvenirs such as T-shirts, videos, books, your own photos and dive log. Items from marine organisms (jewelry, shell, etc.) that are for sale in shops were probably obtained legally, but it is best if these products were never sold at all—it's likely that these items were collected in a non-sustainable fashion and to the detriment of their environment. Sunscreens, clothes, confectionery, film, books, batteries, etc. are available at most resort boutiques and prices aren't too outrageous.

Cane Toads

Despite early warnings by naturalists and scientists, cane toads were deliberately imported into Queensland from South America in 1935 in the Australian Bureau of Sugar's attempt to combat the sugar-cane beetle, whose larvae had devastated the sugar industry. The hope that the beetles would become prime cane toad prey failed when the toads, which can grow up to 15cm (6 inches) long, realized it was easier to dine on other insects and small toads instead of flying beetles.

MICHAEL AW

It wasn't long before everyone realized that nothing was eating the cane toad! In fact, the poisonous glands on the back of the toad's head mean a highly toxic (and deadly) meal for any potential predator. Some birds and animals have now learned how to kill and eat the non-toxic parts of the toad. But the toad's initial lack of natural predator in Australia and its sexual ferocity, which results in females laying up to 35,000 eggs in a single spawn, combined to create an ecological disaster. Today, cane toad populations in Australia are ten times the density than in their native Venezuela.

While the perennial question of how to eliminate the toad remains unanswered, motorists go out of their way to run them over and killing a cane toad is essentially a public service. The cane beetles, by the way, were eventually controlled by pesticides.

Activities & Attractions

PAUL SINCLAIR

Queensland, the "Sunshine State," has an almost endless variety of land- and water-based tourism opportunities. Rainforest excursions and outback activities abound, and excellent accredited ecotourism operators are available in areas all along the Queensland coast. National parks, well-developed information centers and helpful materials make planning easy.

The enormous range of habitats on the GBR—its islands, coast and nearby Coral Sea—offer almost every conceivable watersport activity in addition to diving and snorkeling. Marine parks and other regulatory agencies implement a range of management controls and services, which enhance your safety and enjoyment.

More people are using this region every day; amenities and services change rapidly. Be conscientious and respectful of the environment, plan sensibly and use the appropriate safety equipment—all of which will contribute to your fun.

Island Camping

Pitching a tent on one of the GBR's islands is a unique and affordable way to experience the great outdoors. Facilities range from virtually nothing to showers, composting toilets and picnic tables. Most of the islands are national parks and permits from the Environmental Protection Agency are required. Some are booked out a year in advance, especially during local school holidays.

As the island ecosystems are extremely fragile, campers need to take special care not to upset the balance by following some simple guidelines. Camp only in designated areas and pack all of your garbage out. Some islands are exceedingly remote so plan accordingly. As all plants and animals on the islands are protected, fires are generally banned. Bring a cookstove and, as water is often unavailable, bring your own. Be aware that islands can be isolated by rough weather or strong winds, so bring extra food and water in case you're forced to stay an extra day or two.

Where to Camp

The following islands or island groups are available for camping. Contact the relevant Environmental Protection Agency (EPA) for permits (see page 161 for contact information).

Camping Islands	EPA
Capricorn & Bunkers	Gladstone
Keppel Group	Rockhampton
Cumberland Group	Mackay
Whitsunday Islands	Whitsunday
Orpheus Island	Cardwell
Hinchinbrook Island	Cardwell
Family Islands	Cardwell
Dunk Island	Cardwell
Hope Islands	Cairns
Lizard Island Group	Cairns

Beware the Crocodiles!

Estuarine crocodiles occupy creeks and estuaries along Queensland's coast, and rarely on islands up to 100km (60 miles) out to sea. National parks staff post numerous signs whenever there is a risk of a crocodile encounter.

If you find yourself in crocodile territory (mostly mainland rivers), avoid repetitive behavior and be careful near the water's edge. Although it's the unseen crocodiles that are the problem, don't let the threat of them keep you indoors. There is only one record of a lone research diver being bitten by an estuarine crocodile and that was on an inshore reef rarely visited by recreational divers.

A second species, the freshwater crocodile, occurs in inland freshwater sources. It is smaller and not considered dangerous.

BOB HALSTEAD

Hiking & Island Walking

You can explore excellent hiking trails on the Whitsunday Islands, Hinchinbrook Island and Lizard Island. On the smaller islands you'll find plenty of opportunities to "island walk." About 700 different island walks provide excellent vegetation and wildlife viewing. Some islands and reefs are closed to visitors, so check local marine and national park rules.

The cays in the Swain Reefs area, Capricorn Bunkers, and Bushy Island south of the Whitsundays, as well as many cays farther north, are excellent to explore. Note vegetation differences due to varying amounts of rainfall. Seeds dropped from feeding pigeons can also vastly alter vegetation, as can the coral shingle or rubble substrate of the cay. Some of the rubble cays have mangrove stands—Low, Turtles, Nymph, Hope, Two, Three, Howicks and other islands to the north. Crocodiles have been recorded on several of the far northern cays up to 100km (60 miles) off the coast, so keep your eyes open for tracks.

Mainland or continental islands—including the Whitsundays, Percys, Keppels, Palms, Family, Frankland, Sir Charles Hardy, Forbes, Albanys and others in the Torres Strait—carry unique vegetation, human history and excellent beaches. Your boat skipper will advise you on features of each island.

When visiting any island, stay well away from nesting birds, turtles or other wildlife. Human intervention can create major disturbances to some species. Before stepping on an island, check that you haven't got any seeds in your socks, clothes or shoes. Always carry plenty of water and be sun-safe.

Reef Walking

Many reefs of the GBR expose at low tide at certain times of the year, allowing visitors to walk on the reeftop. Reef walking is the most fantastic way to learn about marine life, especially if you have a naturalist on tap to help you identify various critters and their behavioral patterns. Many organisms you'll see diving also appear on the reeftop—reef walking gives you the luxury of time to observe from another perspective.

There are procedures to follow if you reef walk: basically use common sense, follow the local instructions, avoid damage to you and the substrate and watch the rising tide.

Walking on the Reef

You may ask yourself: Doesn't walking on coral kill it? In some cases yes, but a reeftop is usually a combination of sand grooves, coral patches and "dead" surfaces, which are actually extremely rich algal turfs full of crustaceans and worms. These areas are extremely robust and quite safe to explore with a guide—without a guide it is important to walk in the areas designated by GBRMPA, as some areas are much more fragile than others.

For an enjoyable and successful reef walk, follow these few hints:

- Plan your walk
  - check tide times so you don't get caught out
  - allow one hour each side of low tide
  - tell someone where you are going
  - check local rules
- Wear a hat, long-sleeve shirt, strong shoes and socks to protect your ankles
- Do not touch any animal unless a guide hands it to you
- Use maximum protection sunscreen but be sure not to get it on the animals
- Try using a mask or viewing device to see into deeper water
- Put your camera on a short strap so when you bend over you don't dunk it
- Bring plenty of film

Remember, every surface of the reef has life growing on or in it:

- Always watch carefully where you put your feet
- Walk in sandy tracks between living coral
- Avoid walking near edges of pools, where coral is fragile and can collapse
- If you turn over a boulder, carefully ensure that it goes back the way it was
- Leave reef life alone—remember, touching many organisms can kill them

LEN ZELL

Reef walking is a unique experience. Protect the marine life by heeding special precautions.

Semi-Submersibles

A semi-submersible trip is a great activity for non-diving friends and relatives. "Semi-subs" (in local jargon) took the idea of a glass-bottom boat one step further, adding carpets, air conditioning and windows all around. You'll feel instantly transported to another world as you walk below into this room below sea level. Sit tight and relax while the semi-sub takes you on a unique tour around the local reef bommies and edges.

Most subs are aluminum, with two seats across, while some are larger and more luxurious. They are extremely safe and stay close to the surface as you look out the side windows. A guide gives you a comprehensive commentary and answers ques-

tions about the reef and marine life. You can look through clear or plankton-rich waters, floating by stunning coral, fish, turtles, rays and sharks. All this without getting wet! Be forewarned that semi-subs can be a little nauseating in rough conditions, but the water is usually calm behind reefs and islands. This is an excellent way for non-divers to get a glimpse of what divers experience. Semi-subs operate out of Cairns, Townsville, the Whitsundays, Heron and Green islands. Some large dive boats carry glass-bottom boats or semi-subs on board.

Windsurfing

Windsurfing is a popular activity throughout the GBR. You can rent boards at many mainland and island resorts. Some charter boats and dive boats also carry windsurfing gear.

Be careful windsurfing here. Inexperienced people get so far downwind from their boats or islands that they can't get back. Make sure you have someone watching out for you in case you get into trouble—a mile at sea is a long way to paddle against wind and chop. It is important to have good sun protection, and wear sunglasses with a strap so they won't fall off. Gloves and dive booties will help prevent abrasions.

Parasailing

Parasailing is available at several resorts especially in the Whitsundays, at Airlie Beach, Townsville, Cairns, Port Douglas and at other mainland facilities. It is a great way to get a low aerial perspective of the reef and a great buzz at the same time. The ride out in the speed boat, the rigging up and lift off into the sky are gentle and easy. Bring your camera and get some unrepeatable shots—just make sure your camera is splash-proof and secured. Safety standards are high and laws require equipment to be well maintained.

Joy Flights

Joy flights in helicopters and light aircraft are available from most major centers and resorts and are a fabulous way to get some great pictures and understanding of the reef shapes and sizes. Fly between 9am and 3pm and use a polarizing filter on your camera, along with polarizing sunglasses. Beware the polarizing effect through perspex windows. For certain shots, you may find you have to remove the filter.

Sailing

Cruising—bareboat or crewed—is superb around the Whitsunday Islands (possibly the best in the world) and in some areas around Hinchinbrook Island. You can rent yachts of all sizes and powered vessels at many mainland and offshore resorts. The tourist information centers can help you plan for rentals ahead of time.

Dive operators and some charter planes will pick you up from your vessel and take you for day dive trips on request. Snorkeling is very good all around the Whitsundays and many great swimming beaches are available.

"Get Wet"—Stay Dry

Great Barrier Reef Aquarium

In the heart of Townsville, the aquarium at the Great Barrier Reef Wonderland has a huge main tank with living coral, hundreds of reef fish, sharks, rays and other life. You can walk through a transparent tunnel beneath the tank, marveling at the reef life. A wave machine simulates the ebb and flow of the ocean, while circular currents keep the water moving. There are several smaller tanks and extensive displays (including a slide show) on the life and history of the reef. An Omnimax theater and the Pandora Museum are in the same complex.

GBR Aquarium
2-68 Flinders St.
P.O. Box 1379
Townsville, Qld 4810
☎ 4750 0800
fax 4772 5281
www.aquarium.org.au/

Whale Watching

Whale watching is an activity that leaves people emotionally changed and charged. Several species of whales can be seen on the GBR, especially humpbacks and minke whales. Sperm and Bryde's are less common. The "smaller" whales—including dolphins, porpoises, killer and pilot whales—are much more common, although schools of dolphin are rarely seen underwater.

It is illegal to harass whales in Australia and your boat crew will outline the rules—basically let the whales come to you and let them determine the interaction. Minkes are often viewed off Cairns to Lizard Island in June and July, and humpbacks appear from the southern GBR to Townsville from May to October. Snorkeling with the minkes is a wonderful experience, but don't try to approach them as it usually scares them off. Humpbacks can only be observed from a boat unless you're lucky enough to have a rare underwater encounter.

BOB CHARLTON

Whale-watching trips are an excellent way to learn about whale migration, feeding and breeding patterns.

Diving Health & Safety

LEN ZELL

General Overview

Australia is a remarkably healthy country, considering such a large portion of it lies in the tropics. But because of the heat and intense sun, heat exhaustion, heat stroke and sunburn are some of the most significant health concerns. Take care to use and re-apply sunscreen, wear a hat and drink plenty of liquids. Protect your eyes with sunglasses and consider wearing a dive skin or T-shirt while snorkeling.

Other health concerns include Ross River fever and Dengue fever, viral diseases transmitted by some species of mosquitoes. Outbreaks of this disease, whose symptoms often mimic the flu, have occurred along the coast and are most likely to occur in January and February. The risk of infection is low, but keep your bug dope on hand as there is currently no treatment available for these diseases. Japanese encephalitis is another viral disease worth avoiding. Also transmitted by mosquito, this potentially fatal disease has been spreading through Asia and the Pacific and was recently reported in the Torres Strait islands. Vaccination is not required, but precaution against mosquito bites is strongly recommended.

Pre-Trip Preparation

Your general state of health, diving skill level and specific equipment needs are the three most important factors on any dive trip. This is especially true on the GBR, where you'll contend with strong currents, waves, surges and opportunities to do multiple dives. Honestly assess these factors before you leave and you'll be well on your way to enjoying a successful, safe dive trip.

First, if you're not in shape, start exercising. Second, if you haven't dived for a while (six months is too long) and your skills are rusty, make a local dive with an experienced buddy or take a scuba review course. Finally, inspect your dive gear. Feeling good physically, diving with experience and with reliable equipment will not only increase your safety, but will also enhance your enjoyment underwater.

Pre-trip planning is always wise, but for a scuba trip, it's critical. Be careful not to "get in over your head," so to speak. Standards vary among countries and among dive operations. If you have little diving experience, select a popular resort area or boat that sees a lot of new divers, has modern facilities and provides reliable rental gear. On the other hand, if you're in good shape, dive a lot and have your own gear, you might choose a more remote area or operator that requires greater self-reliance. If you didn't get your skills up, discuss it immediately with the local divemaster so he or she can help you without detracting from the other guests' experiences.

At least a month before you leave, inspect your dive gear. Remember, your regulator should be serviced annually, whether you've used it or not. If you use a dive computer check the battery level and if it's low and you can replace the battery yourself, change it before the trip or buy a spare one to take along. Otherwise, send the computer to the manufacturer for a battery replacement.

If possible, find out if the dive center rents, or can service, the type of gear you own. If not, you might want to take spare parts or even spare gear. A spare mask is always a good idea.

Purchase any additional equipment you might need, such as a dive light and tank marker light for night diving, a line reel for wreck diving, etc. Make sure you have at least a whistle attached to your BC and an alternate air source as they are required by law in Queensland. Add a marker tube (also known as a safety sausage or come-to-me).

About a week before taking off, do a final check of your gear, grease o-rings, check batteries and assemble a save-a-dive kit. This kit should at minimum contain extra mask and fin straps, snorkel keeper, mouthpiece, valve cap, zip ties and o-rings. Don't forget to pack a first-aid kit and medications such as decongestants, ear drops, antihistimines and sea-sickness tablets.

To enter Australia you need no immunizations but it's best to fill your prescriptions before departure as drugs vary.

Diving & Flying

Many divers get to the GBR by plane. While it's fine to dive soon *after* flying, it's important to remember that your last dive should be completed at least 12 hours (some experts advise 24 hours) *before* your flight to minimize the risk of residual nitrogen in the blood that can cause decompression injury.

Tips for Evaluating a Dive Operator

First impressions mean a lot. Does the business appear organized and professionally staffed? Does it prominently display membership of Dive Queensland Inc., Queensland Charter Vessel Association and a dive affiliation such as NAUI, PADI, SSI, etc.? These are good indications that the operation adheres to high standards.

When you come to dive, a well-run business will always have paperwork for you to fill out. At the least, someone should look at your certification card and ask when you last dived. If they want to see your logbook or check basic skills in the water, even better.

Rental equipment should be well-rinsed and stored. If you see sand or salt crystals, watch out. Before starting on your dive, inspect the equipment thoroughly:

LEN ZELL

A good dive operator will always take the time to go over the dive plan, emergency procedures and give you a thorough briefing of dive site conditions and features.

Check the hoses for wear, see that mouthpieces are secure and make sure there is a depth gauge, air pressure gauge and octopus, as required by law in Queensland.

After gearing up and turning on your air, listen for air leaks. Now test your BC: push the power inflator to make sure it functions correctly (and doesn't free-flow); if it fails, get another BC—don't try to inflate it manually; make sure the BC holds air and the auto-overpressure valve functions well. Then purge your regulator a bit and smell the air. It should be odorless. If you detect an oily or otherwise bad odor, try a different tank, then start searching for another operator. In Australia equipment and breathing air must pass regular inspections.

Medical Facilities

Coastal centers have excellent medical support and most resorts have a nurse and nurse's station on site. Boats are equipped with a medical kit, which the crew can use under instruction from a mainland doctor over the radio or telephone. All dive vessels are required by law to have oxygen systems and supplies on board, as well as trained staff.

For non-diving sickness or injury, your operator will direct you to the best local medical facilities. Each major city has a central hospital and 24-hour medical clinics. Pharmacies are always useful for advice about minor problems not requiring prescription drugs.

Diving Emergencies

In the unfortunate event you need a recompression chamber, the one you go to will be coordinated and chosen by the **Diving Emergency Service (DES)** ☎ 800-088-200. The only recompression facility in Queensland is in Townsville. If this chamber is unavailable, the DES will arrange transportation to another recompression facility outside of Queensland. Contact the DES for any diving accident, decompression injury/sickness, embolism, marine sting or envenomization, bite or blackout.

When you call the number, listen to the operator carefully, give your exact location, phone number, call sign and boat or resort name and then calmly explain the circumstances. Ideally, you'll be able to give exact details about the patient: name, location, status, what happened, first aid given, depths, times, symptoms, times of onset, etc. Do not hang up until the operator tells you to. This is a free call 24 hours a day.

For all general emergencies (fire, ambulance and police) call ☎ 000. If you call the number, first state what your emergency is and which service you require. Again, listen to the operator carefully, giving as specific information about the patient and incident as possible. Do not hang up until the operator tells you to. This is a free call 24 hours a day.

If you are at a resort, on a vessel or some other commercial facility, report the situation to the appropriate person. Do not try to take over, as the staff will have locally legislated procedures to follow, which may be different from your training.

DAN

Divers Alert Network (DAN) is an international membership association of individuals and organizations sharing a common interest in diving and safety. It includes **DAN South East Asia and Pacific (DAN SEAP)**, which is an autonomous nonprofit association based in Australia that funds the Australian DES. DAN SEAP's emergency number in Australia is ☎ **800-088-200**.

DAN's 24-hour emergency hotline in North America can be reached at ☎ **919-684-8111** or **919-684-4DAN** (-4326). The latter accepts collect calls in a dive emergency.

DAN does not directly provide medical care; however, it does provide advice on early treatment, evacuation and hyperbaric treatment of diving-related injuries. DAN membership is reasonably priced and includes DAN TravelAssist, a membership benefit, which covers medical air evacuation from anywhere in the world for any illness or injury. For a small additional fee, divers can get secondary insurance coverage for decompression illness. For membership questions (Australia) ☎ 03-98869166, fax 03-9886 9155, (North America) ☎ 800-446-2671 or 919-684-2948 elsewhere. DAN can also be reached at www.dan.ycg.org.

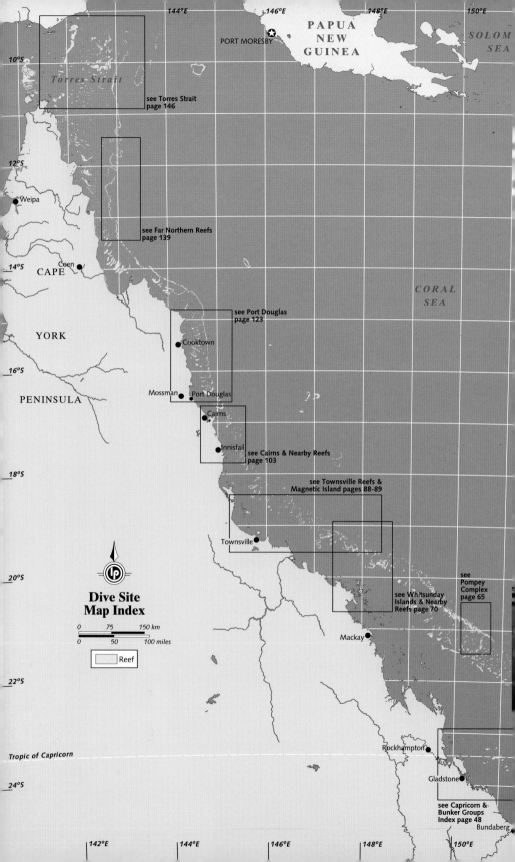

PAPUA
NEW
GUINEA

PORT MORESBY

SOLOMON
SEA

Torres Strait

see Torres Strait
page 146

Weipa

Coen
CAPE

YORK

see Far Northern Reefs
page 139

CORAL
SEA

PENINSULA

see Port Douglas
page 123

Cooktown

Mossman   Port Douglas

Cairns

Innisfail

see Cairns & Nearby Reefs
page 103

see Townsville Reefs &
Magnetic Island pages 88-89

Townsville

see
Pompey
Complex
page 65

see Whitsunday
Islands & Nearby
Reefs page 70

Dive Site
Map Index

0   75   150 km
0   50   100 miles

Reef

Mackay

Rockhampton

Tropic of Capricorn

Gladstone

see Capricorn &
Bunker Groups
Index page 48

Bundaberg

10°S

12°S

14°S

16°S

18°S

20°S

22°S

24°S

142°E   144°E   146°E   148°E   150°E

Diving the Great Barrier Reef

LEN ZELL

Diving the GBR could be a lifelong occupation and even then you would only see a small part of it. The 3,000 reefs and 900 islands—each averaging about 10km (6 miles) of reef edge—mean 30,000km (18,600 miles) of possible dive sites. The inter-reefal sea floors and shoals add another 250,000 sq km (96,600 sq miles) of diveable areas! You'll have an enormous challenge to see even a small part of it.

Linked to the GBR, the Coral Sea reefs, islands and shoals offer another tremendous area of diving and snorkeling potential. The GBR Province is also connected to nearby reefal systems of the Indo-Pacific, which include the eastern Australian coast and Lord Howe Island, through the Torres Straits to the Arafura Sea and Indian Ocean. There are many equally exciting diving and snorkeling opportunities even beyond the GBR.

Shipwrecks stand out as the main "man-made" diving attractions on the GBR and Coral Sea. Queensland has some of the world's best wreck sites—innumerable ships have wrecked on the shallow reefs. Many remain undiscovered, but any wreck that sank more than 75 years ago is automatically protected under legislation. Also protected are wrecks of commissioned Royal Australian navy ships, such as the minesweeper HMAS *Warrnambool*, which was wrecked in 1956 off Cape Grenville.

Mainland river run-off delivers about half as much water to the GBR lagoon as does the rain. The effect of these freshwater masses on reef life can be dramatic, especially on nearshore and fringing reef systems. Run-off is often loaded with silt

Exploring Shipwrecks

Penetration by divers can accelerate a wreck's deterioration. Even minor and inadvertent diver contact can cause structural damage. Divers' bubbles can cause active corrosion of fragile iron structures and bulkheads, especially where protective sediments and marine growths are damaged or disturbed.

Also remember that shipwreck penetration is a skilled specialty that should only be attempted with proper training. Wrecks are often unstable; they can be silty, deep and disorienting. Use an experienced guide to view wreck artifacts and the amazing coral communities that grow on them.

Many ships in the GBR Province are protected historical sites where, among other things, penetration is illegal. Several of the most important wrecks have additional special regulations. Make inquiries at the Museum of Tropical Queensland, 84 Flinders St., Townsville, ☎ 4721 1662.

and chemicals from human activities but seldom extends more than 5km (3 miles) from the coast. Inshore winds keep sediments, stirred up by trawlers or coastal run-off, from settling on the bottom. These conditions contribute to the low visibility often found around Cairns, for example.

Almost all the diving and snorkeling in the GBR is boat-based. Exceptions are Lady Elliot Island, where most diving is done from shore. Some operations have permanent moorings or pontoons anchored at their reef sites, and divers can launch from the pontoons, boats or boat tenders. You can also charter one of Air Whitsunday's planes or other amphibious aircraft and fly to several sites for a dive or snorkel. If you camp on one of the islands and have the gear, you can dive right from the beach.

With such a vast number of excellent sites, diving opportunities are almost limitless. This book's coverage is contained to areas that are dived regularly, are accessible by a commercial operator and are part of the GBR Province.

Managing the Reef

The Great Barrier Reef Marine Park (GBRMP) was established in 1975 and is administered by the Great Barrier Marine Park Authority (GBRMPA). In 1981, the reef was added to the World Heritage List by the United Nations Education, Scientific & Cultural Organization (UNESCO). To date, zoning of 344,000 sq km (132,800 sq miles) has been completed, breaking the GBR into the following primary zones:

General Use A Zone All reasonable uses are permitted including trawling and shipping. Mining, oil drilling, littering, commercial spearfishing and spearfishing with scuba equipment are not permitted in these zones or anywhere in the GBRMP.

General Use B Zone Reasonable recreational and commercial uses are permitted, but not trawling or shipping.

Marine National Park A Zone Recreational use of these areas is permitted, which means fishing with one line and one hook is allowed, but not commercial fishing.

Marine National Park Buffer Zone These provide national-park-like protection, but allow trolling for pelagic fish, and shipping.

Marine National Park B Zone A "look but don't take" zone intended to be kept relatively undisturbed. Fishing and shell collecting are not permitted.

Scientific Research Zone Areas set aside exclusively for scientific research.

Preservation Zone Areas of the reef that are intended to be kept completely untouched. Entry is allowed only in an emergency or for scientific research.

In addition to the primary zones, designated areas reflect temporary changes or status, e.g. special management areas, fisheries experimental areas, replenishment areas, defense areas and seasonal closure for bird or turtle nesting. In any case, always check the zoning of any area before you enter it, especially if you are undertaking any activity that can be classed as extractive or has commercial implications. Information on zoning can be obtained from the authority or through *Reef Notes*, a series of pamphlets produced by the GBRMPA.

Snorkeling

Most reefs and islands are great for snorkeling from boats, beaches and headlands. Most snorkeling is done from boats and pontoons anchored on or near reefs.

It's a good idea to cover up to avoid sunburn. Also be aware of currents, tides and surf—remember that underwater conditions vary significantly from one region, or even site, to another. Seasonal changes can also alter conditions. These differences influence the way you'll dress and what techniques you will use.

ANDY SKIMMING

A snorkeler skims over pink staghorn and table corals.

Live-Aboards

Most live-aboards run scheduled departure trips to offshore reefs from Airlie Beach, Townsville, Cairns and Port Douglas. Trip lengths vary from two to 12 nights. Some operators run a set route to permanant moorings or pontoons, while others are slightly more impromptu. Some boats go on "exploratory" dive trips where, weather and conditions permitting, the boat goes out with an aim to find new sites, which may have never been dived before. It is worth checking out various offers, as some will also offer specialist itineraries following marine life events, such as minke whale or coral spawning, or offer trips to more remote spots such as the far northern reefs, Pompey Complex or Swain Reefs.

The length of trip depends on the vessel's permit and government registration. Most of the dive charter vessels have a "roving permit," which allows them to operate in most of the GBR region and the Coral Sea. Some of the operators also have annual scheduled trips to a special remote area of reefs, so it is worth contacting them to find out what upcoming trips they have planned. Also, operators often have spaces on someone else's charter, which you may be able to slot into last minute, although this is less common and is undependable.

The listing of live-aboard operators (see the Listings section) in this book includes only Dive Queensland members, who follow a set of agreed standards, including a commitment to the industry not seen in all operations.

Several other vessels offer cruises that involve some diving, but diving's not their primary focus. They cruise from Townsville to Cairns or from Cairns to Lizard Island and view good snorkeling and diving as adjuncts to good cruising.

Certification

Diver training facilities are numerous along Queensland's coast. Most islands have their own certification programs or are linked to a facility that does. All follow FAUI, NAUI, SSI, PADI or similar training agency systems. Most GBR operators do a good job—it's just that many do a better job. Things change with new ownership and experience of operation and staff, so do your research well beforehand. If you can, ask other recent students about their experience and find out as much as you can about the operation itself.

The listing of Dive Queensland members shows those that offer instruction from introductory courses to advanced training and other specialties. Upon request and for an extra fee, charter vessels will supply instructors.

The GBR is a great place to learn to dive, but be aware that most diving you will do after this will not compare! It may be better to learn elsewhere and then spend the time here enjoying your new skill.

Many GBR operators offer safe and professional first-time certification and specialty courses.

Pisces Rating System for Dives & Divers

The dive sites in this book are rated according to the following system. These are not absolute ratings but apply to divers at a particular time, diving at a particular place. For instance, someone unfamiliar with prevailing conditions might be considered a novice diver at one dive area, but an intermediate diver at another, more familiar location.

The "Depth Range" given for each site refers to the depth the site is usually dived at. A "+" after the maximum depth indicates that the site has potential to go much deeper. "0m" depth indicates that the reeftop exposes at some low tides but may be 5m under water at high tides. Some sites have more than one rating, indicating that different types of dives are described and available in the area.

Novice: A novice diver should be accompanied by an instructor or divemaster on all dives. A novice diver generally fits the following profile:
◆ basic scuba certification from an internationally recognized certifying agency
◆ dives infrequently (less than one trip a year)
◆ logged fewer than 25 total dives
◆ little or no experience diving in similar waters and conditions
◆ dives no deeper than 18m (60ft)

Intermediate: An intermediate diver generally fits the following profile:
◆ may have participated in some form of continuing diver education
◆ logged between 25 and 100 dives
◆ dives no deeper than 40m (130ft)
◆ has been diving within the last six months in similar waters and conditions

Advanced: An advanced diver generally fits the following profile:
◆ advanced certification
◆ has been diving for more than two years; logged over 100 dives
◆ has been diving in similar waters and conditions within the last six months

Regardless of skill level, you should be in good physical condition and know your limitations. If you are uncertain as to your own level of expertise, ask the advice of a local dive instructor. He or she is best qualified to assess your abilities based on the prevailing dive conditions at any given site. Ultimately you must decide if you are capable of making a particular dive, depending on your level of training, recent experience and physical condition, as well as water conditions at the site. Remember that water conditions can change at any time, even during a dive.

Dive Site Icons

The symbols at the beginning of the dive site descriptions provide a quick summary of some of the following characteristics present at each site:

 Good snorkeling or free-diving site.

 Remains or partial remains of a wreck can be seen at this site.

 Sheer wall or drop-off.

 Deep dive. Features of this dive occur in water deeper than 27m (90ft).

 Strong currents may be encountered at this site.

 Strong surge (the horizontal movement of water caused by waves) may be encountered at this site.

 Drift dive. Because of strong currents and/or difficulty in anchoring, a drift dive is recommended at this site.

 Beach/shore dive. This site can be accessed from shore.

 Poor visibility. The site often has visibility of less than 8m (25ft).

 Caves are a prominent feature of this site. Only experienced cave divers should explore inner cave areas.

Marine preserve. Special regulations apply in this area.

Capricorn & Bunker Groups Dive Sites

As the southern extremity of the GBR, the Capricorn and Bunker reefs and islands (Lady Elliot Island is included in the Bunkers here for convenience) are an unusual but excellent representation of what the GBR and Coral Sea have to offer. There are 21 reefs—13 with vegetated cays (Fairfax and Hoskyn have two cays on one reef), one with a non-vegetated cay, and five significant reefal shoals.

It is possible to camp on Lady Musgrave, Masthead and North

LEN ZELL

Aerial view of Lady Elliot Island

West Islands once you've obtained permits from National Parks. Heron and Lady Elliot Islands are home two of the three coral cay resorts—the third is Green Island off Cairns.

Access to the area is limited. You fly to Lady Elliot from Bundaberg, helicopter or fast catamaran to Heron from Gladstone, and fast catamaran to Lady Musgrave from Bundaberg. Charter vessels journey to the other reefs and islands, departing from, Seventeen Seventy, Bundaberg, Gladstone and Yeppoon.

All the reefs expose on most low tides so there are excellent opportunities to reef walk and snorkel, in addition to the varied diving around all the reefs and shoals. Humpback whales frequent the area from May through October, and manta rays and turtles are seen regularly. Thousands of birds and turtles nest on these islands.

BOB CHARLTON

Look for humpback whales in May through October.

47

One Tree Island and Heron Island are home to research stations, operated by Sydney University and Queensland University respectively. One Tree Reef (off One Tree Island) is closed to recreational use to allow researchers undisturbed work space. Around all the reefs, watch that you don't disturb equipment set up for scientific experiments.

With over 222km (120 nautical miles) of reef edge, innumerable bommies, shoal areas and shallow inter-reefal areas, diving opportunities abound. Each resort has buoyed sites for drift diving, while charter vessels cruise out to their favorite spots. Whatever your need or style of diving, it is available in this area.

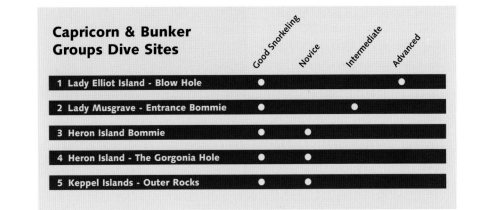

Capricorn & Bunker Groups Dive Sites	Good Snorkeling	Novice	Intermediate	Advanced
1 Lady Elliot Island - Blow Hole	●			●
2 Lady Musgrave - Entrance Bommie	●		●	
3 Heron Island Bommie	●	●		
4 Heron Island - The Gorgonia Hole	●	●		
5 Keppel Islands - Outer Rocks	●	●		

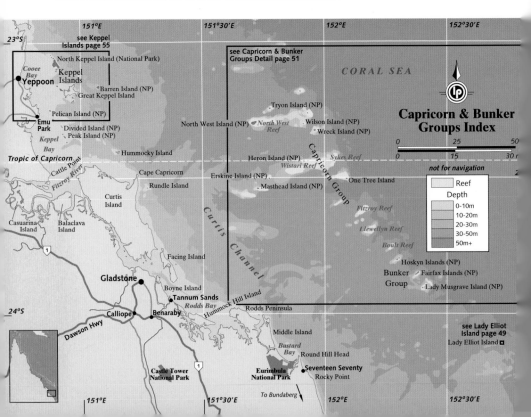

1   Lady Elliot Island - Blow Hole

The resort on Lady Elliot gives you access to the best resort-based diving on the GBR. The visibility is better—although access is more difficult—than at many other sites. The near-circular reef has great snorkeling over the reeftop and edge, and excellent dives at **Lighthouse Bommies, Anchor Bommie, Coral Gardens** and **Encounters.**

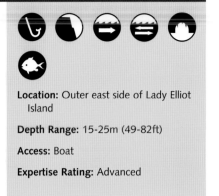

Location: Outer east side of Lady Elliot Island

Depth Range: 15-25m (49-82ft)

Access: Boat

Expertise Rating: Advanced

Looking up at the Blow Hole entrance.

Manta rays are regulars here, along with a resident loggerhead turtle and visiting green turtles. Leopard sharks, moray eels and schools of pelagics make this area enjoyable.

Most diving is from the beach and across the reef flat; sea state and tides restrict boat diving.

An exception is Lady Elliot's most famous dive site, the Blow Hole, where you do a boat entry from the mooring buoy. You drop you onto a reef terrace at 15m, where a hole suddenly appears in the reef. It is only about 6m across and drops vertically into the gloom below.

Formed probably by freshwater erosion during the last ice age, or by wave action as the sea level rose, this great L-shaped geological feature provides a superb dive. The hole turns at right angles at the bottom and travels for 20m before opening out into another hole about 6m wide and 3m high. This opening in the wall is an exciting dive in itself, as it rises from 25 to 15m, running off to the left and right away from the Blow Hole.

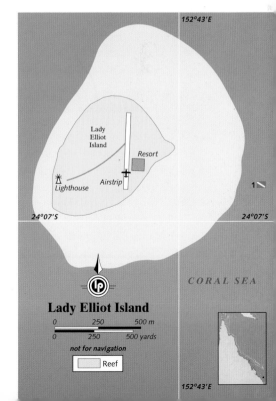

Lady Elliot Island

not for navigation

Reef

After exiting the hole at 25m, the bottom of the wall to the right offers great caves, nooks and crannies occupied by anemones, hard and soft corals, magnificent gorgonians and many fish. Keep a regular look out into the blue as passing manta, eagle and bull rays sometimes accompany the reef sharks and turtles that visit often. Silvertip sharks also sometimes appear. Some regular visitors include lionfish, wobbegong sharks and schooling blubberlips. Wrasse and banded coral shrimp provide cleaner services here. In summer, the hole can fill with clouds of baitfish, attracting predators that come crashing through the masses.

Once you're in the hole, look up for superb silhouette shots, and more photo opportunities as you hit the bottom of the turn. Feather stars and black, turret and soft corals all add color to frame your shots in the tunnels. This is definitely a wide-angle lens dive that requires a computer and multi-level tables. Bring a light to enhance your discoveries.

LEN ZELL

Hungry fish face into the current to capture passing planktonic food.

2 Lady Musgrave - Entrance Bommie

Lady Musgrave, one of 12 vegetated coral cay reefs in the Capricorn and Bunker groups, exemplifies them all. It has some excellent diving along its back edge near the island (where you can camp). Top sites include **Coral Gardens, Battery Bommies, Manta Ray Bommie** and **The Drop-Offs**. The pontoon anchored in the lagoon is an excellent base for great snorkeling all round this reef.

When the tide is rising or slack, the Entrance Bommie is the jewel in this crown of dive sites. It can only be dived

Location: 5km (3 miles) outside entrance to lagoon, northwest side of reef

Depth Range: 5-22m (16-72ft)

Access: Boat

Expertise Rating: Intermediate

by boat and is near the boat entrance to the lagoon. Tides can cause strong currents running in or out of the opening. A roll entry drops you onto the top of this large coral head, which is rich in coral cover. You can dive to a maximum depth of 22m and then work your way up and around the bommie. Numerous small nooks, crannies and overhangs provide lots of places for small marine life to hang out.

Porites, or boulder coral, is the primary constructor of this head, with large colonies of plate and staghorn coral now covering much of the surface. Mushroom and brain corals are also common among the soft corals, which are interspersed throughout the site.

The constant passing parade of fish includes painted flutemouths, clown triggerfish, batfish, sergeant majors, butterflyfish and coral trout. Clouds of blue damsels and passing schools of trevally add to the movement. If you are lucky, lionfish, large cod or giant moray eels may show up. Barramundi cod, big eyes and cardinalfish can be seen hiding under the overhangs.

Manta rays and sea snakes are less common, but keep your eyes peeled as you never know when they'll show up. Turtles visit more regularly, sometimes resting under one of the many overhangs. Don't disturb them; they can slam into you causing you to lose your mouthpiece or mask.

The sea snakes seen here are best observed from a distance—they are inquisitive but highly venomous, although harmless if you don't annoy them. Look for cuttlefish here too—their constantly changing colors add to the kaleidoscope effect of the site. Parrotfish crunch at the coral and algae and at night can be found resting in their mucous cocoons. Whitetip and blacktip reef sharks can appear here as well.

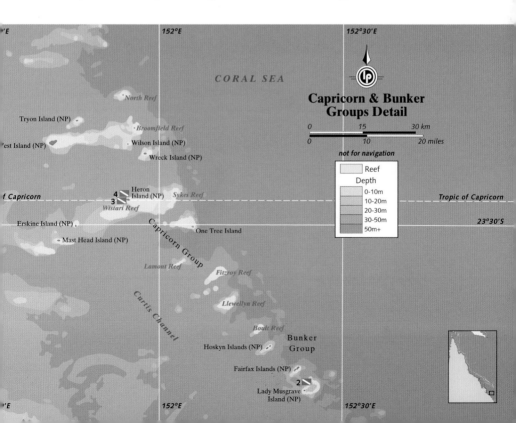

3   Heron Island Bommie

Heron Island is a richly vegetated coral cay with a resort, research station and Marine Parks ranger base. It is an important nesting site for green turtles, black noddy terns and wedge-tailed shearwaters. It is serviced by helicopters and a high-speed catamaran—30 minutes and 2½ hours, respectively, from Gladstone.

Location: Between harbor mouth and west end of reef

Depth Range: 3-25m (10-82ft)

Access: Boat

Expertise Rating: Novice

There are about 10 regularly dived sites with canyons, gullies, bommies, walls, drifts and sandy floors. The Bommie is one of the most famous dive sites in the world, as this area has been seen in almost every film, documentary or story ever done on the GBR and was one of the first regularly dived sites.

It is a very "reliable" site with good access. Schools of hussars and sweetlip, whitetip reef sharks, moray eels and parrotfish swim against a superb backdrop of staghorn coral banks and four large (and many smaller) boulder coral heads. This is also the local cleaning station and is a great place to get the token shot of a cleaner wrasse inside a trout's mouth.

Overhangs and several tunnels provide ideal conditions for turret corals, which come out at night. Notice how they expose their brilliant yellow polyps—quite a switch from their drab orange-brown daytime color. Some fish hang around at night, sleeping in the small caves and overhangs. Don't disturb them. Note the way the colorful butterflyfish and angelfish go quite dull at night, lying around in a daze.

LEN ZELL

A many-spotted sweetlip is joined by a school of hussars.

Keep a good eye out into the blue to see manta and eagle rays, which are regular visitors but hesitate to come close. Often the first divers to the site will see resting turtles at the base of the heads, along with wobbegong sharks.

An anchoring boat broke the top off the main head in the '70s and the constant diving pressure has removed most of the fragile corals from the site. Increased diver-sensitivity seems to be allowing the coral to slowly return. The staghorn bank had some bleaching recently but is still in good shape.

After a giant-stride entry, follow the mooring line down to an old admiralty anchor and then to the largest head in only 6m. You can easily spend your whole dive here or go exploring down the sand slope and around the smaller heads. The current can be uncomfortable on big tide runs. It is a great snorkel site, but can get a bit crowded if the semi-sub shows up at the same time.

4 | Heron Island - The Gorgonia Hole

This site is a boat dive only and has an excellent variety of small soft corals. Like all the sites at Heron, the diverse array of fish is very familiar with divers.

Your dive leads you down a reef slope through several boulder coral heads, gully structures rich with tabulate staghorns, and into a hole-like amphitheater. Then swim over into a broken reef edge with

Location: Due north of resort, on reef slope

Depth Range: 3-25m (10-82ft)

Access: Boat

Expertise Rating: Novice

LEN ZELL

"Micro-atolls" of star and staghorn corals are kept flat by the average low tide height.

numerous small caves, gullies and great coral cover. At 20m, the base of the slope breaks into a sand-rubble floor with isolated coral patches. Stay above this, where the life and scenery is much better.

This is a popular site because you see the full range of soft corals that occur in this part of the world. Farther east along the wall, you'll see larger fan corals and staghorn coral colonies in the shallows. Fern-like stinging hydroids are common.

Turtles are regulars here, especially in summer during mating and nesting periods. Feather stars and their small commensal gobies, shrimp and crabs provide more splashes of color as the basslets and damsels swarm in and out of the corals. Sea fans reach out into the current, while smaller nudibranchs, worms and crabs are seen in close. Trevally, hussars and sweetlip are common here and if you're lucky, you'll see an octopus, shark, manta or eagle ray.

A reef edge dive, this site suits all types of divers and photographers and is generally very safe. If there is a strong current run you may get to see several other nearby sites during a drift dive.

The Turtle's Precarious Birth

Six species of marine turtle are found in the GBR and Coral Sea waters. Most common are green, hawksbill and loggerheads. These species mate in the waters around nesting islands, and the nesting females can be seen ashore at night. You can also see them from the air, from boats or when diving throughout the GBR.

A nesting female lumbering out of the water is a wonderful sight to see. Once on land, she first digs a body pit and then an egg chamber. If the sand temperature and moisture content is right, she will lay between 50 and 150 eggs. She then buries the whole pit area, including the egg chamber, and leaves. She will lay up to five times in one year, but only every three to five years.

Incubation takes about six or seven weeks and then the hatchlings dig up the surface and wait until it is dark and cool (either at night or after a rain shower) before emerging. Sand temperature affects the outcomes of each nesting—hotter sand (above 30°C (86°F)) results in more females, 30°C produces both males and females, and below 30°C more males.

The dash across the beach to sea is dangerous. Seagulls and other predatory birds will swoop in for a meal. Once the turtle escapes and reaches the safety of the water, it becomes prey to sharks and larger fish that will happily feast on it. If it makes the journey,

the turtle cruises the open ocean until it is about dinner-plate size, when it returns to start living in reef waters. Adult turtles regularly travel thousands of kilometers, so those protected in Australia may be hunted or eaten in Indonesia.

If you see a turtle, consider yourself lucky—be respectful of this rare experience. Don't shine flashlights, walk in front of nesting turtles, or go closer than 15m (50ft). Always be slow and careful. Never touch or hang on to turtles underwater, as this stresses them greatly and they may be on their way to the surface to breathe.

LEN ZELL

5 Keppel Islands - Outer Rocks

With two large islands, several smaller islands and rocks, the Keppels area has some great dives on fringing and "veneer" reef communities (where the reef life grows a veneer over island rock). The best dives are at **Outer Rocks, Barren Island, Man & Wife Rocks** and **Egg Rock**.

Your entry at Outer Rocks drops you to 8m, next to some superb ridges rich in hard and soft coral. The coral in this area was partially bleached in the 1998 bleaching event but have recovered well. You can track down and over the ridges to the northeast, turn west over to the point and then back up into the shallows for your safety stop at the end of your dive.

The ridge is known as Snake Paradise due to the resident population of olive sea snakes, which generally appear less

Location: Due east of North Keppel Island

Depth Range: 4-22m (13-72ft)

Access: Boat

Expertise Rating: Novice

inquisitive than their fellow snakes because they are so busy searching for food. If their curiosity gets the best of them, they may check you out on their way to the surface to breathe.

There are many gutters to explore, some with sea cucumbers on the bottom and side ledges. A careful look under the ledges may yield a painted crayfish, sea star or nudibranch sighting. Damsels,

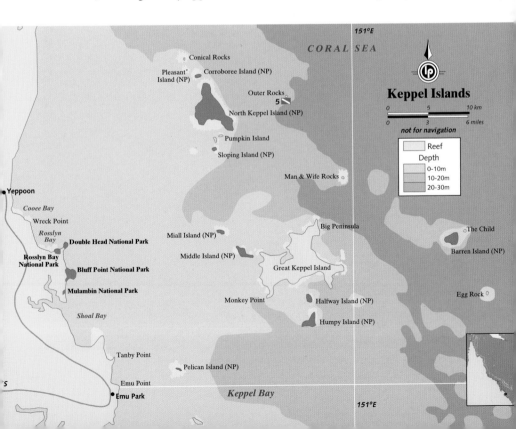

CORAL SEA

151°E

Keppel Islands

0   5   10 km
0   3   6 miles

not for navigation

Reef
Depth
0-10m
10-20m
20-30m

Conical Rocks
Pleasant Island (NP)
Corroboree Island (NP)
Outer Rocks
5
North Keppel Island (NP)
Pumpkin Island
Sloping Island (NP)
Man & Wife Rocks

Yeppoon
Cooee Bay
Wreck Point
Rosslyn Bay
Double Head National Park
Rosslyn Bay National Park
Bluff Point National Park
Mulambin National Park
Shoal Bay
Miall Island (NP)
Middle Island (NP)
Great Keppel Island
Monkey Point
Big Peninsula
The Child
Barren Island (NP)
Egg Rock
Halfway Island (NP)
Humpy Island (NP)
Tanby Point
Pelican Island (NP)
Emu Point
Emu Park
Keppel Bay
151°E

butterflyfish, sergeant majors, fusiliers, anemones, wrasse and parrotfish are always present here. You'll also see coral trout, wobbegong sharks, stingrays and

Olive sea snakes slither around Snake Paradise.

the occasional Maori wrasse. Green and loggerhead turtles are also regular visitors, along with long toms, Spanish mackerel, greasy and honeycomb cod.

The snorkeling and safety stop area is in toward the island, over the staghorn coral patches and up to the rocks, where a moray eel hangs out. Be careful not to rub the oyster-covered rocks that are submerged at high tides—they can cut you badly.

Stinging hydroids, stonefish and lionfish are dangers to be aware of but aren't usually a problem. Best times of year tend to be late winter to early summer when visibility is better, winds and waves milder.

A diver gets a close-up view of an anemone and its resident anemonefish.

Coral Bleaching

LEN ZELL

Abnormally high water temperatures and urban pollution carried through
coastal run-off are two major contributors to coral bleaching.

Coral bleaching occurs when corals are under severe stress, which can be induced by a variety of factors. Extreme temperatures and increased UV rays are the two most important, but disease, chemicals, salinity and exposure to air and rain at extreme low tides can also be significant.

Bleaching occurs when corals shed some or all of their zooxanthellae, the single-celled plant that lives in the coral animal tissue. The colony appears to go white, but if you examine it closely, you'll see a thin layer of animal tissue, like a sheath, over the white calcium carbonate skeleton. Corals can recover if the stress was not extreme and if the few remaining zooxanthellae reproduce and re-establish the symbiotic relationship.

Research shows bleaching to be a regular natural phenomenon that can worsen in El Niño years, with fluctuating water temperatures and tides. Human influences on coastal run-off water quality and low salinity effects can also contribute to coral bleaching.

Recently, on the GBR's inshore fringing reef systems, a major bleaching event was linked to high temperatures, low tides, rainfall, coastal run-off and very calm conditions. Almost 90% of inshore reefs had significant bleaching in 1998, and 25% had more than half their corals affected.

The offshore reef systems of the GBR and Coral Sea had minimal or no bleaching recorded, probably due to less water from the mainland and more water movement, lessening the hot water accumulation seen in shallower coastal waters. Six bleaching events have been documented on the GBR in the last 20 years with anecdotal evidence indicating that more have occurred in the past. There is now major concern that coral bleaching is a strong indication of global warming.

Swain Reefs Dive Sites

LEN ZELL

Exploring a swim-through.

This is the southern extension of the "wilderness and adventure" diving areas of the GBR. It is serviced only by charter boats with "roving" permits. The Swain Reefs complex is 100 to 250km (62 to 155 miles) from the coast and has over 270 reefs—more than 25 have cays. These reefs range in size from a few hundred meters across to over 20km (12 miles) in length. Most average around 4km (2.5 miles), providing thousands of exciting exploratory dive sites. The reefs are rich and the cays important as protected seabird rookeries and resting areas. There's also an automatic weather station on one of the cays.

Today, parts of the Swain Reefs are used for commercial trawling, fishing, recreational use and research. In many areas, recreational and commercial fishing has depleted the

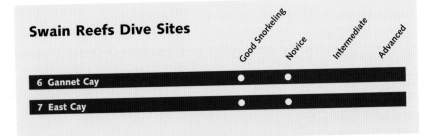

Swain Reefs Dive Sites

	Good Snorkeling	Novice	Intermediate	Advanced
6 Gannet Cay	●	●		
7 East Cay	●	●		

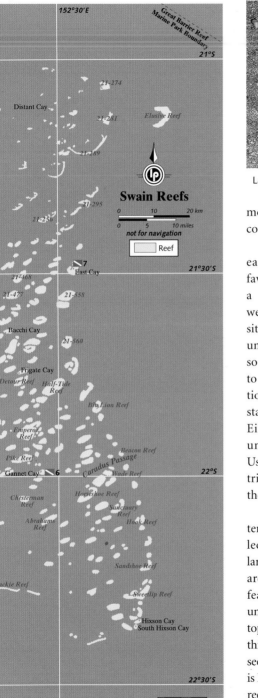

Land hermit crabs thrive on some coral cays.

more popular fish species such as trout, cod and sweetlip.

As much of the area is unexplored, each dive boat takes divers to the favored spots, usually associated with a good anchorage in the prevailing weather. There are many anchorage sites so even if many boats are out, it is unlikely you will see them—the area is so large. Operators generally take divers to either the northern or southern section, depending on what harbor you started from and how long you have. Either way, you will get excellent uncrowded diving and snorkeling. Usually the itinerary is flexible—your trip will be determined by weather and the whim of the group.

Good walls, excellent reef edges, gutters, drop-offs, tunnels, swim-throughs, ledges, terraces, caves, overhangs and large coral heads occur throughout the area. In short, virtually any coral reef feature you can imagine can be seen underwater here. Shallow lagoonal reeftops and sandy floors host large staghorn thickets and many species of shells can be seen, especially at night. Most of the area is less than 30m (100ft) deep between the reefs, so there is not much opportunity for deep diving. Visibility can be reduced during rough weather and big tides.

Sea snakes are common at some reefs, and sharks, turtles and rays can be seen throughout. Fish diversity is high. The usual suites of inshore species abound, with outer-edge species becoming more prevalent as you go east. Whales, whale sharks, dolphins and leatherback turtles have all been reported, so keep your eyes peeled.

Shipwrecks can be seen on some reeftops but many other wrecks are yet to be found. Tales of bravery and sadness abound from ships that sailed, dived and fished this complex.

PHILIPPE GUIQUEL

Keep your eyes peeled for passing spotted eagle rays coming in from the outer edge.

6 Gannet Cay

Gannet Cay is closed during bird nesting periods (summer) and is a national park area. During the rest of the year it is a fascinating place to walk around, checking out the small vegetation and the shape of the island, with its little short cliffs and beautiful sandy beaches, usually covered in nesting birds.

Several large pinnacle-like coral bommies feature as the most popular sites to dive. Sharks are seen regularly, as are sea snakes and turtles. Upon descent to your planned depth you will see large gorgonians, with feather stars perched on their tops. Check both for beautifully colored commensal shrimp, gobies and crabs.

Location: Back reef slope and bommie fields

Depth Range: 1-27m (3-90ft)

Access: Boat to shore

Expertise Rating: Novice

Pelagic fish are common, especially trevally, mackerel and barracuda—usually chopping into the baitfish in early morning or late afternoon. Trout, cod, lionfish, butterflyfish and angelfish are also common. This is a great spot for excellent macro and wide-angle shots.

NEVILLE ZELL

Look for large fan gorgonians throughout the GBR.

7 East Cay

Boat operators are attracted to this reef by the easy-access anchorage and small sand cay. Diving is attractive here due to the variety of reef structures, especially on the north and east ends of the reef. Complex bommies and gutters provide great swim-throughs with sandy floors. Back in the more sheltered areas you'll find rich staghorn thickets and small coral patches. The bommies reach from the sand at 20-25m to the surface.

By diving from a dinghy you can enter the water on either the outside for a drift dive, or in amongst the gutters if the weather or current make it unsuitable to drift. Go to your planned depth and work your way up and around the complex of structures. It is usual to see larger fish like trout, cod and whitetip reef sharks in the gutters. Small angelfish, butterflyfish, damsels and surgeonfish are common, with wrasse and parrotfish

Location: Northeast of back reef slope and bommie fields

Depth Range: 1-25m (3-82ft)

Access: Boat

Expertise Rating: Novice

zipping around as well. Sea snakes are common—they should be treated with respect and left alone.

Feather stars sit up on the fan corals catching passing food. It is easier to photograph molluscs on the sand at night, as they are seldom seen any other time. This site is good for wide-angle photography on most days but is always a great macro area. Numerous varied sites provide for a great snorkel or dive on this reef.

Two remoras join a whitetip reef shark in its quest for food.
Remoras have a flat suction disk on their heads, which enables them to attach to moving fish.

What is a Coral?

Coral is a popular term used for many bottom-dwelling animals. The four main ones are, in evolutionary sequence: **hydroids** (or stinging corals), **anthozoans** (hard or stony corals), **black corals**, and **gorgonians** (including soft corals).

Hard corals are the primary reef-builders and these animals have a major waste problem. As hard corals grow, they dump their waste calcium carbonate crystals outside their tissues. The pattern in which these crystals are laid down leads to the 350 different shapes of hard coral skeletons we see when the coral dies and rots, or is eaten. The zooxanthellae—a single-celled plant that lives inside the coral tissue—absorbs carbon dioxide, waste phosphates and nitrates from the coral (other animals discard the waste through their urine and feces). It also collects sunlight and produces sugars and oxygen that the coral, in turn, uses. During this symbiotic process, calcium carbonate becomes a waste product and has to be dumped. *Voilà*—a coral skeleton.

The coral animal is a polyp—each polyp is an individual and may be joined to thousands of others to form a colony. Each polyp has a sac-like stomach with a ring of tentacles around the top and a mouth in the center. The stomach has internal vertical ridges that help digest food and also carry the gonads. These ridges also generally determine the shape of holes in the coral skeleton.

Coral tentacles are packed with stinging cells called nematocysts. These act like mini-darts, injecting toxin into prey. Corals are farmers by day, when the tentacles are retracted, allowing the zooxanthellae to absorb sunlight. They become active carnivores at night when the tentacles expand and wave around to capture any blundering prey. The prey is taken into the sac-like gut and digested. Hard wastes are ejected out the central mouth, the digested food is shared amongst polyps in the colony and the wastes are used by the zooxanthellae.

Corals are vicious killers and will engulf one another through slow overgrowing, or by sending out sweeper tentacles, which kill or digest neighboring corals. This is a slow process (taking months or even years) but is very effective in the slow and purposeful life of a coral.

Soft corals generally have multiples of eight tentacles and usually a fleshy (filled with spicules or little spines in the tissues), horny or semi-rigid skeleton, such as in sea fans and whips. There are many other corals such as the rare black, red and even freshwater "corals," belonging to quite different groups of animals than the hard and soft corals of the Indo-Pacific reefs.

LEN ZELL

Corals are relentless carnivores, devouring each other in the competition for space.

Pompey Complex Dive Sites

Between the Swain Reefs and Whitsundays, the southern wilderness adventure diving area continues. The Pompey Complex (which includes the Tee Line and Hardline) has blue holes, U-shaped channels with strong currents, sheer walls, water "falls," whirlpools and an unbelievable diversity of reefs. Navigation is dangerous for many vessels, so the area remains underexplored. If you get the chance to get here—take it!

About 150 reefs make up this complex, which is about 200km (124 miles) north-to-south, 90km (56 miles) west-to-east and up to 185km (115 miles) from the mainland coast. Most have no names and are recognized only by their numbers on the Marine Park Zoning Plan maps. Some are 20km- (12 miles-) long, others are square-shaped, up to 100 sq km (40 sq miles). The reeftops have many intricately shaped, closed and shallow lagoons and some are almost flat, abraded coral/algal surfaces. Between the reefs are channels up to 90m- (295ft-) deep and 200m- (656ft-) across. Their U shape was probably formed during the last ice age.

PHIL WOODHEAD

The Pompeys mark the southernmost extent of the beautiful giant clam.

Some of the outflows and many reefs appear as deltas from the air. Their sides are vertical walls that fall to a smooth abraded limestone floor.

The tide change inshore of the Pompeys is the largest on the east coast of Australia—over 9m (30ft)—which means an enormous amount of water passes through here four times each day, on the two rising and two falling tides. It is common to see tide runs in excess of 15km/h (9mph), which cause whirlpools and rising water that is 10 to 20cm (4 to 8 inches) higher than the reef. Tide heights range from 6m (20ft) inside to 4m (13ft) outside of the Pompeys—the highest tide ranges on coral reefs in the world.

As you might expect, the marine life here is rich and hardy, able to withstand intense water speeds. This is the southernmost distribution of the giant clam (*Tridacna gigas*). Sea snakes are common throughout much of the area but where and when they'll appear is unpredictable. The currents ensure great populations of pelagic fish in all the gyre and lee eddy areas.

At least three blue holes occur in this complex. These are usually old caves (formed during the last ice age), which collapsed as the waters rose.

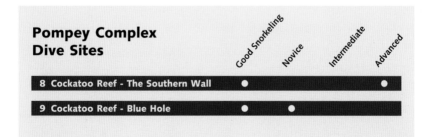

Pompey Complex Dive Sites

	Good Snorkeling	Novice	Intermediate	Advanced
8 Cockatoo Reef - The Southern Wall	●			●
9 Cockatoo Reef - Blue Hole	●	●		

8 Cockatoo Reef - The Southern Wall

An "adrenaline rush" describes this site well. You need to know exactly when the tide stops running, get into the water, enjoy your dive and as soon as you see all the fish turn to face the other direction, end your dive! This means the tides are a-changin' and you really don't want to get caught in running tides. Know your plan and your buddy well and carry your safety sausage.

Location: Channel edge of reef on southern side

Depth Range: 1-27m+ (3-90ft+)

Access: Boat

Expertise Rating: Advanced

These channels have vertical walls that plummet from the reeftop to the floor, which is scoured limestone rock and can be 40-80m deep. In the middle of the reef wall, the life tends to be smaller, obviously adapted to strong water flows. Hard corals, small soft corals, sponges, coralline algae and many small fish abound. Soft corals, gorgonians, feather stars and other filter feeders are common, but again are generally smaller outside the many caves and overhangs. Schools of pelagics also flash through.

Once you reach either a channel into the lagoon, or the end of the reef channel just before a rising tide, drift and pop around into the lagoon or back reef area where another world awaits. Rich staghorn beds and coral gardens, abraded coralline algal surfaces and many grazing fish are the norm.

Sharks, barracuda, rays and mackerel circle in the eddies, awaiting unsuspecting fish. On the lagoon floor, many shells come out—especially at night. Feeding sea cucumbers and goatfish are common.

JOHN BARNETT

When feeding on the bottom, goatfish use their barbels to tickle the sand and sense their food.

9 | Cockatoo Reef - Blue Hole

One of at least three blue holes in the Pompey Complex, this one has the classic shape of a perfectly round coral rim. It sits in a shallow lagoon about 10m deep. The rim exposes at low tide and has a vertical wall to 10m outside and 7m inside, which then slopes inward forming a conical pool with smooth sand and sediment sides.

Location: Inside lagoon

Depth Range: 1-27m (3-90ft)

Access: Boat

Expertise Rating: Novice

Snorkeling around the 200m diameter rim is fun, with rich staghorn corals off on the lagoon floor and lower sides of the wall, and tabulate forms on the outer edge of the wall. Once inside the rim, you'll find a mix of coral species with staghorns becoming more dominant. All coral stops at about 15m as it becomes buried in sediment. It is a fascinating experience to dive in what was a cave thousands of years ago but has since collapsed, forming this pool.

Fish life inside the hole is limited, presumably due to lower water exchange, but you'll still see stripeys, sweetlip, trout, damsels, butterflyfish, wrasse, parrotfish and angels. Outside is a "normal" lagoonal reef edge supporting rich life, especially in the small overhangs and caves. There you'll see worms, crabs, crayfish, shells, soft and hard corals and sea cucumbers.

LEN ZELL

Reeftop stubby corals adapt to pressures from surge and waves.

Baitfish, pink anthias and anemonefish swim among tabletop and boulder corals.

Whitsunday Islands Dive Sites

Over 100 continental islands make up the Whitsundays, including the Cumberland Group and the coast from Mackay to Bowen. The Whitsundays appeared when the seas rose 10,000 years ago, drowning the valleys between the islands. This area is now a tourism hotspot. These islands boast excellent sailing and the biggest bareboat charter fleet in the South Pacific, a jet airport (on Hamilton), great beaches, inlets and fringing reefs. Seven islands have resorts, and camping is permitted on others.

The main accommodations and primary exit points to the area are at Airlie Beach and Shute Harbour, with some from Mackay, Proserpine and Bowen. On the resort islands, which have lodging ranging from hostels to 5-star hotels, there are ample resort-style activities including golf, hiking, tennis, windsurfing and dining.

Divers are serviced by the resort dive shops or by prior arrangement with a dive operator for pick-up at an agreed-upon location. You can even go by float plane on a "champagne flight," landing at the area of your choice where you'll dive and then fly back.

From the Whitsundays, you can dive the local fringing reefs or the GBR proper, which is only 40km (25 miles) east of the islands and has a superb range of dive sites. Humpback whales pass through in winter and the other reef life is rich and diverse. Reef structures are excellent with great walls, caverns, overhangs, coral gardens and lagoons. Strong currents from the big tides are not a problem, as dive operators know where to go, regardless of the conditions.

PHILIPPE CUQUEL

Whitsunday Islands Dive Sites

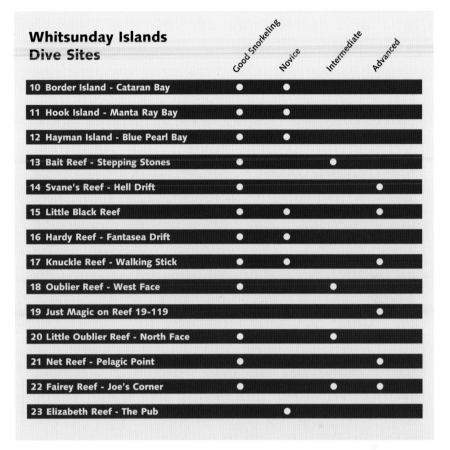

	Good Snorkeling	Novice	Intermediate	Advanced
10 Border Island - Cataran Bay	●	●		
11 Hook Island - Manta Ray Bay	●	●		
12 Hayman Island - Blue Pearl Bay	●	●		
13 Bait Reef - Stepping Stones	●		●	
14 Svane's Reef - Hell Drift	●			●
15 Little Black Reef	●	●		●
16 Hardy Reef - Fantasea Drift	●	●		
17 Knuckle Reef - Walking Stick	●	●		●
18 Oublier Reef - West Face	●		●	
19 Just Magic on Reef 19-119				●
20 Little Oublier Reef - North Face	●		●	
21 Net Reef - Pelagic Point	●			●
22 Fairey Reef - Joe's Corner	●		●	●
23 Elizabeth Reef - The Pub		●		

10   Border Island - Cataran Bay

Being the Whitsunday most distant from the coast, Border Island's visibility tends to be somewhat better than on the inshore islands, although it's still not great. The winds can be strong but the water stays calm enough for snorkeling or diving.

Watch for turtles and, during whale season, listen for the songs of passing humpbacks. Reef sharks are common but spook easily and are quick to disappear. When large schools of baitfish are here, watch as predatory trevally, queenfish and mackerel swoop in for a meal. Fusiliers are common, along with many smaller reef fish that dart among the coral.

Location: North side Border Island

Depth Range: 0-15m (0-49ft)

Access: Boat

Expertise Rating: Novice

You can find excellent walls and overhangs. The areas around and under large bommies provide great hiding spots for coral trout and sweetlips. The shallow areas are dotted with numerous clams in various shades of blue, aqua and purple. Christmas tree worms are also common, as are many other small organisms if you take the time to look for them. This is an ideal site for macrophotography.

On the shallow areas of the bommie tops more soft and hard corals, join large colonies of stinging coral, so beware

their fiery sting. Parrotfish graze on the exposed reef surface and pairs of butter-flyfish dart around between the staghorn coral colonies. As you finish your dive, take a drift snorkel or swim over the shallows to see how different these sites are to other reef types. Snorkeling is best in this area at mid- to low tide.

MICHAEL AW

An underwater photographer glides over a plate coral wall.

11 Hook Island - Manta Ray Bay

Anchoring is prohibited in this bay and the moorings have a two-hour time limit as it is one of the more popular bays in the Whitsundays. The fish are numerous and well-fed—look for Fat

Location: Northeast end of Hook Island

Depth Range: 0-15m (0-49ft)

Access: Boat to shore

Expertise Rating: Novice

Hook Island's crisp coral coastline.

Albert, the resident Maori wrasse, for proof. He weighs in at about 100kg and has bright aqua markings around his face. Smaller females accompany him wherever he goes. Interestingly, when Fat Albert dies, the largest female will frantically change sex and take his place as the dominant male.

Sex Lives of Fish

If you ever asked a fish what sex it was it would be important to add, "I mean, right now." Many fish change sex irreversibly during their growth—some from male to female and some female to male. The cleaner wrasse is a good example. A male has a harem of females. If you remove the male, the largest female, which the male dominated until now, turns into a male. She (he) now dominates all the females and if "he" is removed then next largest female becomes a male, and so on.

The Maori wrasse is the largest wrasse found in GBR waters.

The anemonefish has a different system: One large female lives in a "family" made up of a male and several juveniles. If she is removed, the male becomes female, and the juveniles step up the sex ladder as well.

Obviously, fishing can negatively affect breeding populations. If, for example, a large male coral trout is removed, following the rules of nature, a female then must change sex younger and smaller than it normally would, making reproduction less effective.

When it comes to parenting, fish employ every conceivable method. Some spawn in the surface waters (pelagic spawning), while others spawn on the bottom by attaching their eggs to the substrate and caring for them until they hatch (demersal spawning). Seahorse females lay their eggs in the male's front pouch, where they stay until they hatch. Some sharks give birth to live young, others lay eggs. If you are a tiger shark, your siblings may even eat you before you are born!

Underwater terrain consists of large bommies from 15m to the surface with overhangs, small caves and clumps of corals on a muddy sandy floor. Visibility ranges from 1 to 7 meters. Stinging coral and staghorns give primary cover. Friendly batfish abound with fusiliers, sergeant majors and masses of planktiverous (plankton-eating) fish more common near shore.

The blue staghorn thickets here are probably the best in the Whitsunday Islands. Soft corals, occasional black coral trees and gorgonians can also be seen. If you venture to the rocky end of the bay, look for some of the big splits occuring in the rocks.

Cleaner stations are common and you might see a cleaner swim into Fat Albert's mouth to clean his teeth and gills. On good visibility days this is a great area for macro or super-wide-angle photography. Be careful surfacing as you finish your dive, as boat traffic is common.

Many varieties of coral cling to each other as they compete for space on the sandy floor.

12 Hayman Island - Blue Pearl Bay

The Whitsunday Islands are surrounded by an abundance of rich fringing reefs, sandy and rocky shores and mangroves. The northern islands tend to have clearer waters, although the reefs are generally the same species composition. Popular sites include **Maureen's Cove**, **Manta Ray Bay** and **Butterfly Bay**. Snorkeling at any of these island beaches, coves and reefs is a delight.

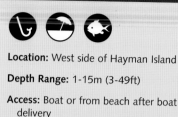

Location: West side of Hayman Island

Depth Range: 1-15m (3-49ft)

Access: Boat or from beach after boat delivery

Expertise Rating: Novice

Blue Pearl Bay has fringing reef diving at its best. The visibility is never that great, but the diversity of life is outstanding. Large coral heads rise from the muddy sand floor at 7 to 15m and are topped with delightful aggregations of sergeant majors, blue pullers and other damselfish, which dash about the stinging and plate coral colonies.

A resident tasseled wobbegong shark is hard to find because of its camouflaged skin and habit of lying under small overhangs. Batfish, harlequin tuskfish and parrotfish are abundant with the territorial damsel likely to rush out and peck your hair as you approach its territory.

Small caves, overhangs and crevices through the bommies occur but few, if any, are safe to swim through. The sizes are restrictive and the silt stirs up easily. Keep your buoyancy; the silt gets bad if you hang out near the bottom.

During the day, notice the coral here has incredibly long, out-stretched polyps, especially the long-tentacled mushroom corals, which often have commensal shrimp grazing on their tentacles. Anemones are common, hosting several species of clownfish. Observant divers will be well rewarded with sightings of nudibranchs, carnation corals and other unusual life.

As you finish your dive in the shallows watch out for the many stinging coral colonies, which are also common throughout the dive. Boat traffic can be a worry so always be aware of where and how you ascend.

LEN ZELL

Tasseled wobbegong sharks use their fine teeth to eat fish and crabs.

13 Bait Reef - Stepping Stones

Bait Reef is the first reef you'll encounter as you head east of the Whitsunday Islands. It has several diving areas. The Stepping Stones site includes **The Maze, Cluster of Four, Coral Gardens, Hawaii** and **The Looking Glass**. The Stones are a series of 17 flat-topped bommies that expose at low tide; seven more round-topped bommies are submerged. You can dive here for a week and still not see it all.

Romance Bommie (and nearby reef edge) is a comfortable night and day dive with a sandy floor and walls on the edge. The bommie is adorned with a large hump of coral that has several swim-throughs.

You start this dive among the stones by dropping in near one of the bommies to 20m, only a few meters up-current from the shallow coral edge. Great swim-throughs, splits, gullies, overhangs and crevices are all around. Below them a sand slope starts at 15 to 23m and slopes away past 30m. Lower down the rubble

Location: Southwest back of Bait Reef

Depth Range: 2-27m+ (7-90ft+)

Access: Boat

Expertise Rating: Intermediate

slope there is less hard coral cover, colonies of spiky soft coral and sea fans.

As you are almost always surrounded by bommies, you can get caught in lots of amazing eddy effects. It is great fun to use the eddies to swoosh around to

LEN ZELL
Swim-through opening onto staghorn thickets.

CRAIG LAMOTTE
Aerial view of the Stepping Stones.

the other side of a bommie, then wait for the water to change direction and take you back.

A great scattering of staghorn clumps leads to thickets on the shallower lagoon side, and soft corals decorate the ridges below the bommies. Look in the thickets for foxface, anemones, butterflyfish and angelfish. Mushroom corals lie around under the coral trout, sweetlip and whip corals. Occasionally you'll see a turtle asleep under an overhang or feeding on the edges of the bommies.

Swim-throughs, gullies, overhangs and a rich set of reeftops provide good diving and ideal fish habitats. Feather stars give a splash of color and schools of fusiliers hover in the current, feeding and waiting for night when they become more active. This is a great macro site and, on clear days, wide-angle opportunities are fantastic.

14 Svane's Reef - Hell Drift

This is an exciting parachute-entry dive that tests your buoyancy and general diving skills—you need to get yourself together, collect your buddy and swim over to the vertical reef edge before you begin the drift along it. In parts, the reeftop is heavily reticulated with gullies and grooves giving superb coral coverage for hovering fish that take refuge from predators and the current.

Once you reach the reef edge, drop down the wall to your planned depth and be careful you don't go past it as it is very easy to do so. It is probably not worth it as the life drops off quickly after 20m. Gorgonian fans, whips and sponges with clinging feather stars are

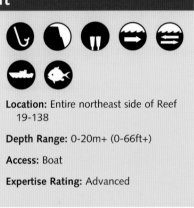

Location: Entire northeast side of Reef 19-138

Depth Range: 0-20m+ (0-66ft+)

Access: Boat

Expertise Rating: Advanced

colorful features here. Large fish species like trout, sweetlip and cod are common with pelagic mackerel and trevally zooming past. Up the wall and in the shallows, masses of smaller planktivores flit about and you may spot turtles cruising by.

A great way to do this dive is to get to a comfortable depth, stay close to the wall, relax and let it all go by while keeping your buddy in view. There is ample life of all kinds and interesting structural features to give you a great dive for minimal effort.

As you finish your dive in the shallows at **Turtle Point**, watch the fish behavior during your safety stop, then surface and swim out to the boat.

LEN ZELL

A shrimp camouflages into a feather star.

15 Little Black Reef

The sandy lagoon floor—at 10 to 20m—has patches of staghorn coral and sea cucumbers, and is a great easy dive or training area. However, the **Elephant Rock** wall dive, on the outside of the lagoon along the reef edge, is definitely for advanced divers.

Location: West side of reef

Depth Range: Lagoon: 20m (66ft); Outside: 40m+ (130ft+)

Access: Boat

Expertise Rating: Lagoon: Novice; Outside: Advanced

Colorful parrotfish abound and the reeftops offer great snorkeling. Inside the lagoon, stingrays are often seen in the sand, and a large bommie provides good all-around diving.

The lagoon walls are mainly vertical with some undercuts and overhangs. Advanced divers can drift the walls and slopes outside the entrance as part of their lagoon dive. South of the mooring, a great night dive takes you along the wall, into the notch and swim-through.

Outside the lagoon the diving is current-driven and tidally dependent. There is the potential to go deep quickly if you don't watch your depth—keep your eye on your gauge, the wall and reef edge. Good corals and fish, overhangs, walls and sand flowing down the rubble slope make this a great dive.

Visibility varies from 10 to 25m. Currents can be quick so trust your dive operator to pick the safest and best times and follow their advice.

Colorful parrotfish use their sharp teeth to chomp away at the coral.

LEN ZELL

16 Hardy Reef - Fantasea Drift

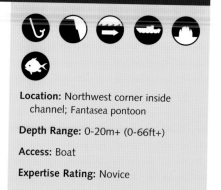

Hardy Reef is a spectacular 13km-long reef with a suspended lagoon and three "waterfalls" that drain it. There is an 80m-deep channel that runs a hundred meters across between Hardy, Hook and Line reefs. Other sites provide enormous overhangs, rich fronts and tops, fascinating lagoons and edges of all sorts.

Location: Northwest corner inside channel; Fantasea pontoon

Depth Range: 0-20m+ (0-66ft+)

Access: Boat

Expertise Rating: Novice

Diving from the Fantasea pontoon, Reefworld, is very comfortable. A flat-decked tender from the pontoon drops you up-current to the north or south, depending on the tide, at a buoy with a descent line. You drift with the tide until you hit the mooring line and take the diver ascent line back to the pontoon. All dives are escorted and a lifeguard sits high on the end of the pontoon, watching out for snorkelers and divers.

Small bommies provide great surfaces for anemones and their fish. The scenery consists of both soft and hard corals, massive boulder coral heads up to 5m across, and black coral trees. These are interspersed with encrusting and staghorn corals, gorgonian fans and a host of colorful soft corals. Observant divers can find queen murex, baler and spider shells, plus pincushion seastars, flatworms and an incredible variety of nudibranchs.

Tame fish life abounds along the wall. Mackerel and trevally compete for your attention, along with more colorful reef fish such as butterflyfish,

LEN ZELL

A semi-sub hovers over the Fantasea Drift wall.

angelfish and clown trigger-fish. Turtles are also seen on most dives.

The reeftop is flat with heavily grooved edges that give way to walls and overhangs. These lead down to 10m or 30m, followed by a sand and rubble slope that drops away to 65m. The life is by far best above 20m.

When divers reach the pontoon a rope trail leads to the safety stop under a suspended dive cage. Giant trevally and sometimes George, the resident groper, will be there. Life on the underside of the pontoon is fantastic for macro and wide-angle photography.

Landlubbers watch from the Fantasea pontoon.

17 Knuckle Reef - Walking Stick

A superb anchorage spot, this reef site is shaped like, you guessed it, a walking stick. Inside the lagoon is an easy site for snorkelers and divers, as long as you watch your depth. Outside the lagoon is more suitable for advanced divers. Your entry and exit locations will be determined by the ebbing or flooding of the tide.

An easy drift dive takes you down a wall to 20m, where a slope quickly drops below 40m. At the base of the wall (at the stick "handle"), there is an enormous overhang about 10m high and wide.

Shoaling fish hover along the wall, where fan corals reach out into the strong currents for plankton. Look for the resident hump-headed wrasse in the channel on the northern part of the site, along with passing mackerel and trout.

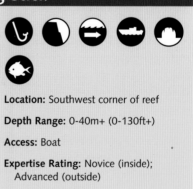

Location: Southwest corner of reef

Depth Range: 0-40m+ (0-130ft+)

Access: Boat

Expertise Rating: Novice (inside); Advanced (outside)

These fish can be seen whether you're snorkeling or diving. Visibility here ranges from 10 to 25m, averaging about 15m. Take your time at this site, as the many smaller overhangs, nooks and crannies provide hideaways for cuttlefish and other cryptic critters. At night, look for sea cucumbers with their commensal animals and shells on the sandy floor.

18 Oublier Reef - West Face

You can get a good dive anywhere on the 9km outer edge of this almost circular reef that has walls, overhangs, gullies and slopes. It also has a rich top and a good lagoon for snorkeling.

To dive the West Face, you enter off the boat into 10m, over coral and sand where you'll start the drift. Carved out by water during the last ice age, this area provides an interesting dive over rolling coral ridges gullied with sand wedges. Although the deeper life is interesting, there is really no need to go below 20m.

Large fish tend to hide under the coral plates and small overhangs, with coral trout and sweetlip being the most common. Look for small life like nudibranchs, shells, sponges, flatworms and lace corals.

Gorgonian fans and whip corals occur on the ridges and the sand provides excellent resting grounds for

Location: Western wall of reef

Depth Range: 0-20m (0-66ft)

Access: Boat

Expertise Rating: Intermediate

rays and whitetip reef sharks when they are around.

Strong currents can occur so you need to keep the reef edge in sight—an unlikely problem with average visibility of 20m. If you do encounter poor visibility, you may need to use your compass, although the bottom shapes are also good for orientation.

At the end of your dive, complete your safety stop on the reef edge and then surface before swimming out to the boat.

Whip corals, feather stars and gorgonian fans grow on the ridge tops.

19 Just Magic on Reef 19-119

An exciting drift dive when you can get to it, Just Magic lives up to its name. Your parachute hot boat entry drops you in about 20m from the reef and you must swim straight in to the edge or risk being carried away when the tides are running. Carry a safety sausage and listen to the divermaster's brief, as it is quite possible to wash off the end of the reef when you're finishing the dive. Remember, you may need to do a mid-water safety stop.

Location: Both sides of Reef 19-119

Depth Range: 1-20m+ (3-66ft+)

Access: Boat

Expertise Rating: Advanced

This is an almost linear but small reef loaded with spectacular coral and fish life. You have the option to swim deep or stay shallower, above 20m, where the life is more interesting. You need to watch your depth constantly as you are against a vertical wall, which juts to and fro on a sixty-degree slope. The bottom is well beyond 40m. Nearer the surface, the wall has a right angle shoulder that gives over to the reeftop, which exposes on extreme low tides.

This colorful site has almost 100% coral cover with spectacular formations, especially branching and table forms of the staghorn group. Larger fish include passing mackerel, tuna, trevally and barracuda. Clouds of blue pullers and other planktivores cruise all over the coral—great for wide-angle photography.

LEN ZELL
Blue pullers dash in and out of staghorn corals.

Coral Cuts

Corals have a mucous-covered surface that is rich in bacteria and fungi. When you cut or scratch yourself on coral, pieces of the coral can break off in the wound, along with the mucous, and severe infections often result.

If you ever have a coral cut, scrub the wound vigorously with a nailbrush or toothbrush using Hibiclens or other antiseptic cleanser. Pour hydrogen peroxide on the wound and let it dry out. Get immediate medical attention if there is continued pain or reddening. Treatment may be difficult as many of these organisms are resistant to antibiotics, so get to it early.

20 Little Oublier Reef - North Face

A roll entry from the dinghy or parachute entry from the main boat takes you to the reef edge and a safe depth of about 18m. The wall on the way down, is rich in coral—delightful inlets or embayments into the reef allow you to swim into beautiful coral gardens of plates and stags in clumps and thickets. There are also covered swim-throughs and caves, but be careful as they can be restrictive and dangerous. Ample sandy floors are good for divers with buoyancy problems.

You may see hump-headed wrasse or gropers, although pelagic species like mackerel are more common. Turtles and whitetips sharks are here half the time.

Location: Northern wall of reef

Depth Range: 0-18m+ (0-59ft+)

Access: Boat

Expertise Rating: Intermediate

As you complete the dive in the sandy-floored northwest corner of the reef, the shallows allow a 5m safety stop in more of the rich coral gardens, with clouds of plankton-feeding fish.

LEN ZELL

Plate and staghorn corals compete for space in the shallow coral gardens.

21 Net Reef - Pelagic Point

A boat tender will take you to your point of entry, just inside the Pelagic Point bommie. You drop in to about 10m and swim into the current until it picks you up and takes you into an eddy teeming with schooling pelagics. These fish always seem to be here, hanging around for the right food to drift into sight. Grey reef sharks regularly visit here as well. This area is also suitable for manta rays, which come to feed on the clouds of planktonic food.

Location: Southwest corner of reef

Depth Range: 0-10m+ (0-33ft+)

Access: Boat

Expertise Rating: Advanced

LEN ZELL
A diver reads her depth gauge during a safety stop.

Once you're through the pelagics, with the current, watching for two bommies coming to within 5m of the surface—keep the deep water on your right. Just after the bommies you'll see the first gap into the shallower areas. Be careful with your depths along here and if the tide run is strong, keep close watch for gushing water in the gaps between bommies. Tuck in to the leeward side of the bommies if you want a break from the current.

By staying on the outside, you will see more of the bigger fish; inside the bommie line, between the 10m-deep gaps, the life is less spectacular. Large gorgonians abound outside, along with big coral trout. This is recognized as one of the best sites in this type of mid-shelf reef area. A choice of safety stops allows you to finish the dive in comfort.

22 Fairey Reef - Joe's Corner

An easy snorkeling and safe dive site starts at Joe's Corner on the flood tide and drifts along a vertical wall, but at 20m slopes quickly away beyond 50m. The wall breaks into a series of bommies linked by a coral-covered floor at 15m. Spectacular corals and fish decorate the reeftop and bommies. If the current run is fast you soon pop around the corner into the sandy-floored lagoon at about 15m, where another dive site, **The Vee**, is an easier dive for beginners.

Joe's has diverse life and is fun because of the mixture of wall and bommie diving—there's an excellent split in the first bommie you encounter. If you must dive on the ebb tide, use the bommies both as a rest from the current and as indicators to turn into the shallower sand floor at

Location: Northwest corner of reef

Depth Range: 0-20m+ (0-66ft+)

Access: Boat

Expertise Rating: Intermediate or Advanced

15m. Otherwise you may get swept along and off the wall past the corner.

The currents out here lead to more pelagic species of fish, good gorgonian fan corals and, if you are extremely lucky, the odd manta ray or turtle may venture past. Many small patches of staghorn, small bommies and coral clumps grow in the shallows. Look out for painted crayfish or the territorial damsels.

LEN ZELL

Egg cowries, seen here feeding on leathery soft corals, are recognizable by their pure white shells.

Tabletop and staghorns dominate at Fairey.

With visibility averaging 15m and ranging from 10 to 25m, you'll see many rarer passing pelagics and good macro subjects, like sea cucumbers and their commensals, moving among the gobies and shrimp in the sandy lagoon. This is a great night dive and you can enjoy either the floor or wall life. When the visibility is good, there are plenty of wide-angle possibilities. Regardless, it is always a guaranteed high-yield macro site.

Always watch the currents and keep the wall or bommies in sight to keep from dropping deep down the slope. This is not a site for learning divers unless accompanied by an experienced guide.

23 Elizabeth Reef - The Pub

Elizabeth exhibits many features of the Coral Sea reefs found farther off the continental shelf. It has excellent visibility and dive sites, including **Gucci Point**.

At The Pub, the tender drops you near the edge of a 20m-wide bommie. This dive is a classic isolated bommie dive—you can circumnavigate it as quickly or as often as you like, or take your time doing slow spirals.

Explore the rich overhangs on the north side or take a swim-through to the east side. Large fish—sweetlips, cod and trout—often hang out in the swim-through. A giant clam sits near the

Location: Northwest end of reef

Depth Range: 0-27m (0-90ft)

Access: Boat

Expertise Rating: Novice

bommie base at 15m, surrounded by a great patch of anemones and clownfish.

A delightful canyon on the south side is rich in fusiliers, baitfish, parrotfish, wrasse, trout, chaetodonts, Moorish idols and passing mackerel. Turtles sometimes appear and pufferfish hover around—don't annoy them as they can easily bite off the end of your finger.

Complete your dive by spiraling upwards, keeping an eye out for blue-banded clownfish in the anemones. As you approach 5m, look up and see the clouds of small planktivorous fish, fusiliers and trevally. This is an easy dive and a good site for all photography types.

Redthroat sweetlip are often extremely curious.

Townsville & Magnetic Island Dive Sites

The third largest city in Queensland, Townsville is the aquatic facilities center, home to the Museum of Tropical Queensland, GBR Aquarium, Australian Institute of Marine Science, GBRMPA and James Cook University. It is a fascinating city, with a bustling mining and agricultural port, a defense forces base and a casino.

Due to their convenient location in roughly the middle of the GBR, Townsville and Magnetic Island have plenty of dining and accommodations options for all budgets, and a smorgasbord of diving opportunities. Many dive operators run from here, servicing the *Yongala*, Coral Sea and nearby reefs. Daytrips to Kelso Reef, three-day cruises to Cairns and live-aboard dive expeditions are also available.

LEN ZELL

The Olgas coral garden at Kelso Reef provides a great backdrop for wide-angle photos.

The Palm Islands to the north are mainland-type islands with good fringing reefs, much like Magnetic Island's, but better due to their greater length. Orpheus Island has a resort and James Cook University's research station. Still farther north, Dunk Island, Hinchinbrook Island and Bedarra Island resorts are serviced from Townsville, Cardwell and Mission Beach.

Reefs off Townsville are diverse and offer a great variety of diving. From Townsville you can also reach the *Yongala* and *Gothenberg* shipwrecks, plus many others that remain unidentified.

Courting masked boobies on Flinders Reef.

Townsville has a hyperbaric medicine unit and the only recompression chamber available in Queensland, so if you're going to get bent, it is best to do it here!

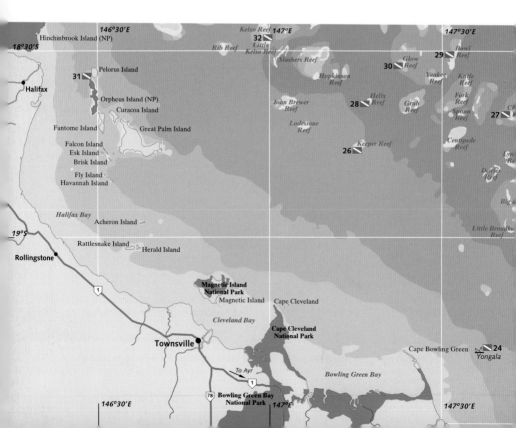

Townsville Dive Sites

	Good Snorkeling	Novice	Intermediate	Advanced
24 *Yongala*				●
25 Lion Reef			●	
26 Keeper Reef - Forbidden City	●	●		
27 Chicken Reef - Split Ends	●	●		
28 Helix Reef - High Voltage	●	●		
29 Bowl Reef - AIMS Bommie	●	●		
30 Glow Reef - Morning Glory	●	●		●
31 Pelorus Island	●	●		
32 Kelso Reef - The Wall	●		●	
33 Flinders Reef - China Wall	●			●

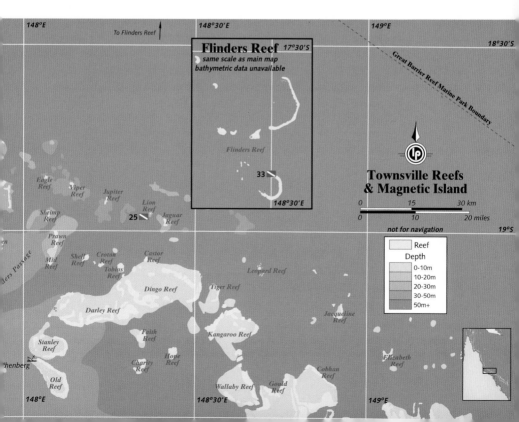

24 *Yongala*

The *Yongala* is undoubtedly Queensland's best wreck dive site. A passenger and general cargo steamer lost in a cyclone in 1911, the *Yongala* was headed to Cairns on her usual run along the Queensland coast. The ship departed Mackay Harbour without telegraph equipment and was too far out before it could be warned of the oncoming cyclone. Details of the ship's sinking are unknown, but it was likely swamped by massive waves that left its 121 crew members and passengers no way to escape the watery grave. Toilet bowls, dinner plates and bed frames still lay scattered in and around the wreck, along with human bones.

The *Yongala* is a significant cultural site and is protected under both the GBR Marine Park regulations and the Commonwealth Government's Historic Shipwrecks Act (1976). Regulations prohibit any activity that is likely to damage the fabric of the wreck or unduly disturb the prolific (and very spectacular) flora and fauna that has colonized the sunken hull. This includes activities such as removing artifacts and spearing fish.

Location: 13km (8 miles) east of Cape Bowling Green

Depth Range: 15-33m (49-108ft)

Access: Boat

Expertise Rating: Advanced

The wreck rests 24km off Cape Bowling Green and can be reached from Townsville or Airlie Beach. Several operators offer tours. If you visit the *Yongala* on a charter vessel you will be briefed about the dos and don'ts. If you dive from a private vessel, you'll need a permit to enter the protected zone. The permit lists conditions and codes of conduct for diving on all historic wrecks off Queensland.

The boat attaches to a buoy and you follow a descent line down. Access to this site is weather and permission dependent—tide runs and sea state can make it a hazardous dive.

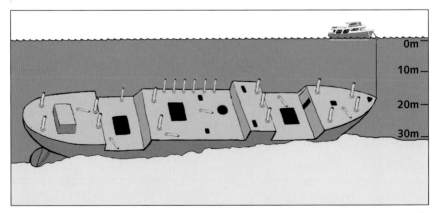

Historians believe the *Yongala* sank bow-first and when the stern came crashing down, she rolled onto her starboard side. Permanent moorings are now established at both ends of the wreck.

The *Yongala*'s coral-covered davits show the prolific life seen all over the wreck.

The port side of the vessel comes into view first and if the current is running you can "hide" in the lee of the hull and work your dive from there. As the entire hull is richly encrusted with soft and hard corals, hydroids, and fan and whip gorgonians, it is a superb macro site. The cruising schools of kingfish, trevally, turrum and barracuda provide for good wide-angle shots. Sea snakes are common, as are bull rays, eagle rays, turtles and enormous groper. One groper, usually found under the bow or stern, is called Vee Dub—it is as big as a Volkswagon!

Oysters line the wreck's interior and underside, leaving dead shell piles on the sand. This 110m-long, and 88-year-old grave is truly an historical oasis in a "desert" of sand—it deserves its total protection. Some say the *Yongala* is the best wreck dive in the world.

Ghost Ship

Details about the *Yongala*'s demise are vague. Most likely, huge cyclonic waves flooded her decks in the early hours of March 24, 1911, leaving her no escape as she rolled under the weight of the water.

Once the raging storm subsided and the *Yongala*, on her 99th voyage with the Adelaide Steamship Company, had still not arrived in Cairns, concern about her seeming "disappearance" grew. Some speculated the ship had anchored off a remote island to wait out the storm. Other steamships came trickling into port, days late, why couldn't the *Yongala*? Families of the ship's 121 passengers kept their eyes peeled on the horizon, hoping the steamship would, at any moment, come slinking into the harbor.

Some of the ship's cargo washed up on shore, but still no trace of the passengers or the ship itself. As days passed and search efforts proved fruitless, hope for *Yongala*'s survival slowly diminished.

Over the years, reports of "mystery sightings" came up empty. Clues to the ship's whereabouts were scarce, until midway through WWII, when a Navy minesweeper located an object, assumed to be a ship-wreck, off Cape Bowling Green. Oddly enough, no further investigation ensued. Finally, in 1958, almost 50 years after the *Yongala*'s disappearance, two Australians investigated the wreck. Sure enough, the word *Yongala* was still visible on the ship's port side. The ghost ship had been found.

The *Gothenberg*

Another protected historic wreck, accessible from Townsville and Airlie Beach, is the *Gothenberg* (maximum depth 18m (60ft)), lost on Old Reef off Bowen in 1875.

Soon after the *Gothenberg* was wrecked, a salvage diver named Dunwoodie, who was working for Capt. William Collins, one of Queensland's pioneer salvors, reported that he had fallen through a thicket of coral and tumbled into a deep abyss while working around the wreck. To date no other divers have reported this abyss, so perhaps Dunwoodie was a little affected by narcosis that day!

Although not as spectacular nor as challenging as the *Yongala*, the *Gothenberg* is an interesting dive and in a better location for novices to practice wreck diving skills. There isn't much of the complete structure left intact, but you will get a good idea of how the wreck broke open as it disintegrated, revealing its large boilers and machinery. If you dive the *Gothenberg*, keep your eyes open and buoyancy right anyway, just in case old Dunwoodie was right.

25 Lion Reef

A small reef with superb diving, Lion Reef experiences some tidal current—enough to make it a little uncomfortable but still worth the effort. Upon entering the water, you have 40m under the boat but shallows on the reef in front of you. Go forward and then, depending on current or your dive plan, work your way around the ten or more bommies that sit on a terrace sloping up from a deep sandy floor.

Fish life is amazing. Schools of giant trevally, Heller's barracuda, Spanish

Location: Southwest side of reef

Depth Range: 5-40m (16-130ft)

Access: Boat

Expertise Rating: Intermediate

mackerel and large trout chase the clouds of baitfish. Fusiliers and damsels pluck plankton from the waters all around the bommies. Whitetip reef sharks can often be seen resting on the sand or disappearing around a bommie.

Feather stars and fan corals reach out into the current to capture their food. These glorious flowing creatures put the "icing on the cake" of rich coral colonies. Painted crayfish can be seen under overhangs as their

Trevally herding scores of baitfish over a bommie.

long white antennae give them away to the observant diver, especially at night. Look for rays on the sandy bottoms, and for the rare black cowtail ray cruising between the bommies.

If you work the current right, you should be able to finish your dive up in the shallows near the reef edge, and then have a nice shallow swim or snorkel back to the boat.

26 Keeper Reef - Forbidden City

Keeper has a great wall dive at **Star Picket** in addition to Forbidden City, where a maze of bommies provides constantly changing opportunities for every diver. This is an easy site to navigate and has excellent vertical walls and edges on the bommies, staghorn thickets and a variety of corals and fish.

After hitting the bottom at about 16m, you have several directions to choose from—you can go down and north a little to the **Elusive Bommie**, or east, where a bommie maze allows you to take spectacular wide-angle shots. Or you can simply concentrate on the macro life anywhere you choose. Continue along the outer edges of the heads, slowly working up and inwards—you will get to see a lot.

As you move between the heads and over staghorn patches take time to look deep into them at the fish, crabs and other life. Note that these staghorns have a single polyp at the end of each branch, as do the little branches of the tabletop corals—this identifies both as belonging to the staghorn group, or genus *Acropora*. There are also some classic plate coral colonies here—look at them

Location: Small bay at south end of reef

Depth Range: 12-18m (39-59ft)

Access: Boat

Expertise Rating: Novice

from all directions, noting how they grow and where the living tissue stops at the base.

Look for open-water pelagics. Parrotfish are common; their falling cloud of feces shows how much coral they crush up to get their food. Plankton-feeding species like damsels and fusiliers are also common and will swarm down into the coral as you exhale. Coral trout, butterflyfish and angelfish swim among the large anemones and their resident clownfish.

LEN ZELL

A cloud of feeding damsels hovers over a staghorn clump.

27 Chicken Reef - Split Ends

Location: South/southwest side of reef

Depth Range: 5-25m (16-82ft)

Access: Boat

Expertise Rating: Novice or Advanced

Diving this site can be both easy as pie or a real challenge to the advanced diver depending on which way you go. Entry into the diverse maze of swim-throughs, caves and caverns should not be attempted unless you are properly trained and sufficiently prepared. The bottom is well covered in coral and life; you need to have your buoyancy under control so you don't damage the reef.

The bottom under Mike Ball's *Watersport* (the only boat that regularly services this site) is at 23m, so dropping in off the dive platform lets you swim forward toward the reef, and then to the left where you'll encounter the first bommie. Go around it and to the right a little and you'll come across the main bommie. This one has a swim-through that branches off to the right in the middle and then exits out the reeftop. You need mid- to high tide to get sufficient water over the reef.

Once you have used up adrenaline in the swim-throughs, take a swim around the bommies, all of which are richly covered in plate, brain, golfball and boulder hard corals, algae and soft corals. This is a good site for macrophotography, as nudibranchs, anemones with clownfish, cleaner shrimp, juvenile fish and many other small examples of marine life thrive. Clams are scattered around the bottom and among the corals, so take time to check out their different colors.

Once you have explored the deeper sections of the bommies, you can spiral up them, using your trip back to the boat as the safety stop. When you are in the open water sections, keep an eye out for the occasional passing turtle or ray.

Red spiky and brown leathery soft corals often provide homes for commensal shrimp.

28 Helix Reef - High Voltage

Helix has numerous good sites, chock-full of great life, gullies and overhangs. High Voltage is excellent for all levels as it has a sandy floor, plenty of depth ranges and an incredible array of swim-throughs and caves that form mazes of coral passageways.

Location: Southwest corner near anchorage and lagoon

Depth Range: 5-27m (16-90ft)

Access: Boat

Expertise Rating: Novice

Entry takes you in to about 20m, and you can easily swim to one of the nearby bommies. On your left, about five bommies have a network of swim-throughs between them. Most are open to the top so light is good and they are generally safe. As you proceed through, try to avoid fin, hose and gauge damage to the corals. One swim-through cave tracks from 16m in a spiral and exits at 6m. As you exit each swim-through you come to a vista of beautiful staghorn thickets and many types of fish.

Large giant clams are well spaced around the site and are as varied in color as the fish. Damsels, butterflyfish, fusiliers, soldierfish, trout and cod are common, with parrotfish and wrasse adding a rainbow of color.

If you tire of the beauty of the bommies and mazes then cross the staghorn thickets toward the reef. On your right

you'll come across **Broken Bommie**. This leads over the reef edge, to another swim-through, between the reef and bommie. From here you can continue along the edge of the reef that surrounds a sandy lagoon area, and then back to the boat.

JOHN BARNETT

Soldierfish hide in caves or under overhangs by day, but come out to feed at night.

29 Bowl Reef - AIMS Bommie

A large bommie, used for research by the Australian Institute of Marine Science (AIMS), was first publicized by its staff. The best feature is a large cave—"The Cathedral"—which opens on the top of the bommie and exits on the western side in 19m. If you are with someone who knows the site, he or she can take you in and then out the top, but watch your safety stop depths and plan well.

Location: Southwest side of large back reef bommie

Depth Range: 1-27m (3-90ft)

Access: Boat

Expertise Rating: Novice

Watch for large fish, lace corals, the black coral near the exit, worms, sponges and sea squirts.

This bommie is surrounded by sandy floors and slopes covered with scattered smaller bommies. On the east side, the slope base is at 24m, 9 to 12m on the southern side, and down to 30m on the western side. Advanced divers can explore the short swim-throughs all over this bommie, which is covered in great examples of big brain coral. As you go deeper, gorgonian fan corals start around 20m.

Some damage has occurred on the north end but the rest of the site is in good shape. The coral diversity is high and it's worth spending time getting a handle on the differences between species. This assumes you are able to tear your eyes away from the little critters that thrive in these dark places.

Up to four large groper have been seen at once but they remain fairly timid and generally keep away from divers. Large schools of baitfish abound, providing food for the cruising mackerel and trevally. Damsels, fusiliers, butterflyfish and angelfish are common and lionfish can be seen in some of the crevices.

Spiky soft and stinging corals hang off the wall at The Cathedral.

30 Glow Reef - Morning Glory

This large bommie and another nearby are detached from the main reef by a sandy floor and scattered coral patches. Both are well covered with rich stands of soft and hard corals and enable all divers to have a dive suited to their experience. Plan your dive well and stick with the plan here.

Below the boat you'll find a large staghorn patch on a sandy floor. Drop down onto the sand and get your buoyancy sorted out, then look over the stag thicket for the life within it. Swim over to the bommie and check out the cave, numerous overhangs and crevices. Lots of small reef life under the overhangs and just inside the cave will keep you occupied for ages. Try to not exhale in the cave as the bubbles can kill rooftop organisms. As you move up and around the bommie, keep an eye out for barracuda, mackerel, trevally and the occasional shark or turtle coming in from deeper water.

More experienced divers may dive off onto the second bommie to the west. It comes to within 6m of the surface and drops away to 36m on its western face. It

Location: West side of main reef

Depth Range: 12-36m (39-118ft)

Access: Boat

Expertise Rating: Novice or Advanced

is as rich as the shallower bommie and has many interesting nooks and crannies. Watch your air and plan your safety stop well. Currents can be a small problem here so watch for them on big tides.

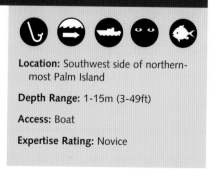

LEN ZELL
Beware: air bubbles from your regulator can kill life in caves or under overhangs.

31 Pelorus Island

Pelorus Island is the northernmost of the Palm Islands. This group of mainland islands boasts a mixture of habitats, from sandy and muddy beaches and bottoms, to rich fringing reefs, mangroves and rocky shores. Many of the fringing reefs have excellent diving.

Accessing the Pelorus site is easy—fall off the *Coral Princess* pontoon into about 3m and then dive to your plan, either up-current and drifting back to the pontoon or setting up a drift-and-dinghy

Location: Southwest side of northern-most Palm Island

Depth Range: 1-15m (3-49ft)

Access: Boat

Expertise Rating: Novice

pickup. Snorkelers can enjoy the excellent fringing reef, nearby white sandy beach and, visibility willing, great viewing all around.

An established feeding station has been set up here at 5m, so the fish are tame and usually waiting impatiently for divers. Sergeant majors, monocle bream, moon wrasse, rabbitfish, red emperor, harlequin tuskfish and the occasional moray eel all gather for the feed.

After the feeding frenzy, follow the slope along the reef edge. This fringing reef is rich due to the mud, sand, current and depths. You can travel at anywhere from 5 to 15m depth and have a great dive. Soft, gorgonian, fan, whip, hard, mushroom and stinging corals are present here.

Bull, eagle and Kuhl's rays can often be seen cruising around or resting on the bottom. Pelagics are here but are usually hard to see in the lower visibility. Beware the stinging hydroids, which look deceptively tame with their beautiful white feather or delicate brown and white hard colonies—they deliver a painful sting when they are touched.

LEN ZELL

Low visibility sometimes plagues the Palm Islands, but the coral coverage is still excellent.

32 Kelso Reef - The Wall

Kelso Reef has six primary dive sites including **The Keg, 2 Buoys, The Olgas** and **Fishing Bommie**. The Wall is an excellent wall and reef slope dive with delightfully rich coral communities.

A giant-stride entry from the Pure Pleasure dive tender drops you into 15m. When you angle in and hit the reef slope at this depth, you can continue deeper down the slope or go up. Below 15m the coral and fish life drops off, more sand and rubble comes in and you'll spot intermittent small coral heads, at about 27m. This site requires good buoyancy—the life is so rich that a crashing diver is almost guaranteed to damage the coral.

Wide-angle photographers can shoot healthy blue and brown staghorns, gorgonians, whip corals, pink sea stars,

Location: Southeast end of reef

Depth Range: 2-27m (7-90ft)

Access: Boat

Expertise Rating: Intermediate

sponges, stinging coral and hydroids. Look also for crown-of-thorns, giant clams, parrotfish and the ever present clouds of blue pullers and yellow damsels. Bump-headed and blue parrotfish are often seen here as well.

Pelagics include trevally, long toms and mackerel, all cruising by off the reef edge. Small towers of coral and larger bommies are interspersed along the

LEN ZELL

Fireweed, feather stars and staghorn corals provide plenty to photograph.

slope as you go north and up onto the shallower areas. Every few meters photographers and videographers will find another "classic reef shot." Large boulder coral colonies, brain and golf ball corals are all over.

Your dive finishes with a safety stop in a shallow amphitheater of staghorns that are surrounded by coral heads. Snorkelers will have a great time in this area as the pontoon is moored near an area of excellent corals.

The Coral Reef Orgasm

Once a year you'll see the coral reefs of the GBR and Coral Sea lying around smoking cigarettes. You guessed it—you just missed the night of the coral reef orgasm. It is on this erotic evening that most of the corals sexually reproduce for the year.

Only in the last decade has sexual reproduction in corals become well understood. We now know that a series of "windows" must be open for this reproduction to occur: warm waters, tides, a few nights after the first full moon of summer, long days, etc.

During spring and early summer a lot of coral energy is directed to the formation of their gametes. Some are single-sex colonies, others are hermaphroditic, having both sexes. The gametes are bundled together on the ridges of tissue in the gut of the coral and then, on the chosen night, these bundles are pushed up to the mouth. This has been described as an upside-down snowstorm as thousands of pink, cream, yellow and red egg bundles are released over a period of hours.

LEN ZELL

The gametes float to the surface where they break up and fertilization occurs. How they recognize their own species is not yet understood. The larva forms and swims directly to the bottom or stays in the plankton for many days. Once it settles on a bottom with the right characteristics, the larva forms a single limey cup, divides into two, then into four, etc. The continuous vegetative reproduction of coral colony growth begins. Some grow into ball shapes, some are encrusting and the fastest growing "weed" species, grow into branching colonies, which can grow up to 15cm (6 inches) per year.

33 Flinders Reef - China Wall

Flinders Reef is an atoll about 37km long and 28km wide. It has a cay and weather tower and represents Coral Sea diving at its best. China Wall is one of the best dives you can have on Flinders, Dart, Abington and Shark Reefs, although each has its own unique features. On most of these reefs the walls drop away to more than 305m.

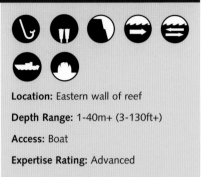

Location: Eastern wall of reef

Depth Range: 1-40m+ (3-130ft+)

Access: Boat

Expertise Rating: Advanced

Good fish diversity occurs in the shallows where emperor angelfish, clown triggerfish and schools of goatfish feed on the sand. Bump-headed parrotfish are regularly seen with pelagic surgeons, dogtooth tuna, trevally and barracuda. Prowlers include silvertip, grey and whitetip reef sharks. On a good day you will also see lionfish and Pavo razorfish, which hide by hovering vertically in the staghorn coral thickets.

Hard corals are small, slow-growing and found in more protected grooves or on the reeftop. You'll see staghorns and tabulates, in addition to golf ball and brain types. Stinging corals are common, with their light brownish-to-white colonies growing in bizarre shapes. Softs and gorgonians are also present.

Many critters can be found in the wall's crevices and overhangs, especially lace corals, sponges, small clams, nudibranchs, morays, anemones and feather stars. Night diving brings out more crabs, shrimps and enormous basket stars.

Caves, caverns and swim-throughs are all along these walls, just waiting to be explored. Sometimes manta rays and hammerhead sharks appear, along with schooling hammerheads in the deep cold water during winter. Some people are lucky enough to see billfish here as well.

Nesting seabirds rest while the sun sets on Flinders Reef.

LEN ZELL

Cairns Dive Sites

Cairns is a true tourism center. With nearby reef, rainforest and outback facilities, it allows anyone with a shorter time frame to "do it all" from one convenient location. Truly a tropical city, Cairns has all a visitor could ask for: an excellent range of accommodations, dining establishments, a casino, shopping and many tour operations.

The nearby rainforest-clad Great Dividing Range is an excellent backdrop to this harbor city. Whitewater rafting, fishing, calm-water mangrove cruises, rainforest tours, helicopter flights, diving and snorkeling daytrips, extended trips or charters are all for the asking.

Your choice of diving and snorkeling excursions from Cairns is amazing. If you have limited time, it's best to book before you leave home as it can occasionally be difficult to get the trip you want. If you start preparing ahead of time, you'll have the opportunity to shop around to find the trip that best suits your needs.

Reefs and islands just offshore are excellent. Green Island is a well-developed coral cay tourist spot, with good snorkeling and diving. It is serviced by several operators. Fitzroy Island is a mainland island with good fringing reefs. Most other islands are visited on daytrips only. Also close to shore is Michaelmas Reef, an internationally significant bird rookery.

PHILIPPE GUIQUEL

A giant feather star clings to a gorgonian fan.

Reefs off Innisfail to the south are quite different from those off Cairns, which are again quite different from reefs off Port Douglas to the north, the start of the Ribbon Reefs. The Innisfail reefs are more broken-up into isolated coral patches; off Cairns the reefs become more solid, and the Ribbons are elongated shelf-edge shapes. Diving or snorkeling on all of them is excellent.

Trips from Cairns access the Coral Sea, Far Northern reefs and Port Douglas to Lizard Island. Some operators invite you to go out on a day boat and then stay overnight at the reef on a "mother ship," which moves daily from reef to reef. Many operators have permanent moorings at sites around Cairns, making the diving easy and accessible. Excellent snorkeling is available at every site.

Cairns Dive Sites

	Good Snorkeling	Novice	Intermediate	Advanced
34 Gilbey Reef	●	●		
35 Coates Reef	●		●	
36 Briggs Reef	●	●		●
37 Moore Reef	●	●		
38 Thetford Reef	●		●	
39 Milln Reef - Three Sisters	●		●	
40 Flynn Reef - Coral Gardens	●	●		
41 Upolu Reef - Lugger's Lagoon	●	●		
42 Michaelmas Reef	●	●		
43 Breaking Patches	●	●		
44 Holmes Reef - Amazing	●			●
45 Holmes Reef - Nonki	●			●
46 Hastings Reef - The Fish Bowl	●	●		
47 Saxon Reef	●	●		
48 Norman Reef - Troppo Lounge	●	●		

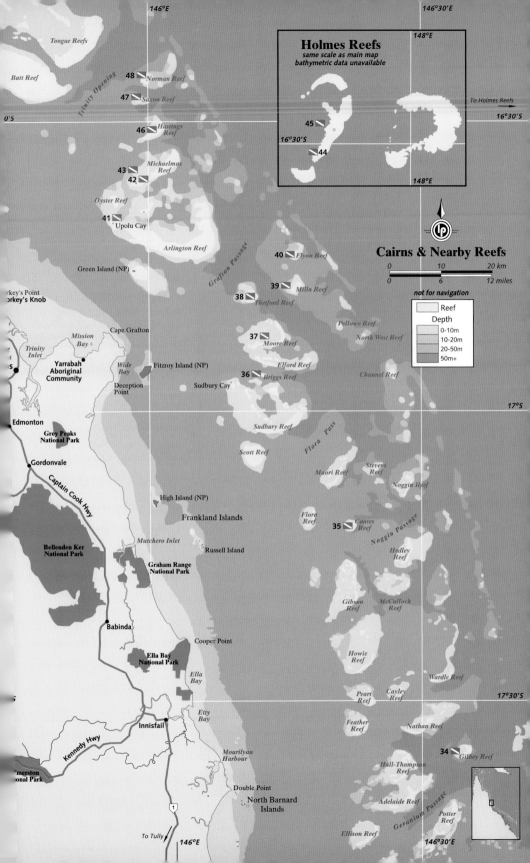

Tongue Reefs

Batt Reef

Norman Reef **48**

Trinity Opening

Saxon Reef **47**

46 Hastings Reef

Michaelmas Reef **43**
42

Oyster Reef

41 Upolu Cay

Arlington Reef

Green Island (NP)

Grafton Passage

40 Flynn Reef

39 Milln Reef

38 Thetford Reef

Pellowe Reef

North West Reef

37 Moore Reef

Elford Reef

36 Briggs Reef

Channel Reef

Sudbury Cay

Sudbury Reef

Flora Pass

Scott Reef

Maori Reef

Stevens Reef

Noggin Reef

Flora Reef

35 Coates Reef

Noggin Passage

Hedley Reef

Gibson Reef

McCulloch Reef

Howie Reef

Wardle Reef

Peart Reef

Cayley Reef

Feather Reef

Nathan Reef

34 Gilbey Reef

Hall-Thompson Reef

Adelaide Reef

Geranium Passage

Potter Reef

Ellison Reef

Holmes Reefs
same scale as main map
bathymetric data unavailable

To Holmes Reefs

45

16°30'S

44

Cairns & Nearby Reefs

0   10   20 km

0   6   12 miles

not for navigation

Reef

Depth

0-10m

10-20m

20-50m

50m+

Turkey's Point
Turkey's Knob

Cape Grafton

Mission Bay

Yarrabah Aboriginal Community

Wide Bay

Fitzroy Island (NP)

Deception Point

Trinity Inlet

Edmonton

Grey Peaks National Park

Gordonvale

Captain Cook Hwy

High Island (NP)

Frankland Islands

Bellenden Ker National Park

Mutchero Inlet

Russell Island

Graham Range National Park

Babinda

Cooper Point

Ella Bay National Park

Ella Bay

Etty Bay

Kennedy Hwy

Innisfail

Mourilyan Harbour

Palmerston National Park

Double Point

North Barnard Islands

To Tully

146°E

146°E

146°30'E

148°E

148°E

16°30'S

17°S

17°30'S

146°30'E

34 Gilbey Reef

A giant-stride entry directly off the dive platform takes you down to the sandy bottom at 8 to 18m, where you can get sorted out before heading off to explore a delightful bommie. You can go either way around this bommie, which has several good swim-throughs on its northern side. There is plenty of depth for most divers, but you can explore at whatever depth suits you. Be careful on the outside

Location: *Coral Princess* mooring

Depth Range: 1-18m+ (3-59ft+)

Access: Boat

Expertise Rating: Novice

where it drops away to 40m—the best life is above 18m.

Giant clams up to a meter long aggregate among the staghorn gardens that grow between the coral heads and the reef. Smaller specimens have iridescent mantles, which make excellent subjects of great close-up and wide-angle photographs.

Anemones with their clownfish, blue chromis, damsels, butterflyfish, emperor angelfish, coral trout, cod, footballer trout and fusiliers are just some of the fish seen here. Pelagics are common with mackerel, barracuda and trevally predominating. Stay around the coral heads, enjoy your 5m safety stop, and you're sure to have a great dive.

LEN ZELL

Turquoise giant clams and blue sea stars stand out on the back reef slopes and sand patches.

35 | Coates Reef

Drop from the *Coral Princess* mooring to a sandy bottom at 8 to 16m. This site is superb for divers and snorkelers alike, although diving with a guide is recommended as the numerous channels and swim-throughs make it easy to get disoriented. Several large coral heads and numerous smaller ones provide excellent substrates for myriad reef life. The dive brief at this site is important, so heed it well.

Schools of fish swim in and above the swim-throughs. Look for sweetlip, apparently sleeping, in the gullies and under overhangs. The outer edge of the swim-throughs has an exquisite array of plate coral canyons. Your buoyancy control is of utmost importance during this part of the dive. More experienced divers can go deeper, although shallower life is better.

Location: *Coral Princess* mooring

Depth Range: 1-27m (3-90ft)

Access: Boat

Expertise Rating: Intermediate

Blue-and-gold fusiliers and damselfish schools hover above the coral. Coral trout, cod, butterflyfish and angelfish also are common. Sporadic sightings of razorfish occur among the staghorn thickets.

Large boulder and other coral heads are interspersed throughout the staghorn and coral patches. The white sand bottom always adds to the sunny brightness of this site.

LEN ZELL

A large boulder coral head dwarfs a snorkeler.
Notice the base of the coral, where sand has been washed away by currents and tides.

36 Briggs Reef

Your skills and training will determine the way you start this dive. Going forward from the bow of the boat will take you over a sandy floor at 11m. Look for the coral head to your left and, farther in, the reef edge has a wall down to sand at 6m. By working along the edge to the left, you'll see good life forms in the small gullies and crevices.

More advanced divers will go out from the stern of the boat and follow a line of six large (and many smaller) bommies, which runs along the edge of

LEN ZELL

Keep an eye open for resident green turtles.

Location: Reeftel mooring

Depth Range: 1-25m (3-82ft)

Access: Boat

Expertise Rating: Novice or Advanced

an 11m terrace that slopes away to 24m. The bommies and reef edge have rich softs and hard coral stands, with staghorn thicket patches interspersed. Feeding sea cucumbers line the sandy floor. Nudibranchs, Christmas tree worms and feather and sea stars also make this a great night dive. Fan and whip corals are common over the edge, on the protected sides of the bommies and in the few swim-throughs.

Whitetip reef sharks are regular visitors, as are wrasse, parrotfish, damsels, butterflyfish, angelfish, rabbitfish and surgeonfish. On lucky days you'll see green turtles. As you swim over the sandy areas watch for blue-spotted rays and seasonal manta ray visits.

37 Moore Reef

Several operators run trips out to Moore Reef, a large reef rich with life. Operators mostly work the back reef areas, all of which have similar dives.

Each dive takes you over staghorn thickets on sand that slopes out and drops to 22m. You can go out right or left to the bommies, or stay closer to the reef edge. Some of the bommies have great swim-throughs and the smaller bommies are also well worth exploring. As you swim out, watch for rays buried in the sand.

Location: Sunlover Cruises mooring

Depth Range: 1-25m (3-82ft)

Access: Boat

Expertise Rating: Novice

Gullies in the reef side make excellent sites for fish observation. The larger bommies usually come to within a few meters of the surface so you can dive at whatever depth you feel most comfortable. At night you'll see nudibranchs, crabs, worms and outstretched coral polyps. Also look for the occasional crayfish.

The abundant hard coral is in good condition and well interspersed. The soft corals hide damselfish, which dash out to catch planktonic food. Wrasse are common, along with parrotfish, emperors, butterflyfish and surgeonfish. A school of grey reef sharks has been spotted here, but you'll more likely see a whitetip reef shark resting on the sand. This is proba-

bly best as a macrophotography site—especially at night, but you can also get the odd wide-angle shot.

LEN ZELL

Cowtail rays are usually timid around divers.

38 Thetford Reef

An almost 2km-long reef with scattered coral heads along its back (leeward) edge, Thetford boasts numerous dive sites. Be careful of your navigation here and take along a safety sausage as it is easy to become disoriented, only to find yourself well away from the boat with no time left.

Sandy floors in between the numerous coral bommies are covered with smaller coral patches and numerous blue staghorn thickets. Look among these for giant clams, butterflyfish, rabbitfish, damsels, angelfish and the occasional

Location: Bommie fields, northwest side of reef

Depth Range: 1-25m (3-82ft)

Access: Boat

Expertise Rating: Intermediate

pipefish. Moving over to the bommies, you'll be confronted with many swimthroughs—most are partially closed on top, sending magical shafts of light down into these mysterious passageways.

The large gorgonian fans and soft corals in these tunnels need special care so watch your fins. Anemones host several species of commensal fish and beautiful transparent shrimps cavorting in their tentacles. As always, it is the slow and observant diver who will get to see them.

JOHN BARNETT

Colorful Christmas tree worms decorate the reeftop.

Some of the boulder coral heads have dozens of multi-colored Christmas tree worms. The bright whorls of their brachial plumes make them look like little pairs of Christmas trees. These whorls are used for feeding and breathing. If you get too close, the polychaete worm will retract into its tube in the coral, pulling a cap over its end for protection.

A fish-feeding permit allows the *Coral Princess* to attract trevally, wrasse, spangled emperor, red bass, blue-and-gold fusiliers and sergeant majors for the benefit of guests.

39 Milln Reef - Three Sisters

The Three Sisters are a series of three large bommies lined up at the back of Milln Reef. The deepest rises from about 33m off sand on the northwest side, and comes to within a meter of the surface. The other two, closer inshore on an easterly bearing, are shallower with the innermost bommie in about 14m off a sand and rubble bottom.

Location: Reeftel mooring at Milln Reef

Depth Range: 1-33m (3-108ft)

Access: Boat

Expertise Rating: Intermediate

If there is little current, start your first dive on the deepest bommie, which has steep sides and is capped by giant schools of fusiliers, various snappers and chub. As you go down the walls, you'll see barracuda hanging silently in the blue. At the bottom, coral trout and cod move in and out of the overhangs and crevices. A superb stand of black coral on the deepest side of the bommie is home to commensal gobies.

In good visibility, you may be able to see the second sister, about 40m to the

MICHAEL COLLINS

The underbelly of a wave as it breaks over a Milln Reef bommie.

east. After spiraling up the first large bommie, head east. You will likely see several whitetip sharks resting on the sand. They will lazily swim away if you approach, only to return minutes later.

A green turtle has made Three Sisters its favorite haunt, and is often seen hanging near the surface around the second sister, where it feeds on sponges and algae. The depth at the second sister is about 19m; explore around the base, where you are likely to see more sharks, blue-spotted rays and other sand dwellers.

Upon approaching the third sister, you'll be confronted by one of those memorable sights of diving: the walls between sisters two and three are straight-sided and only about 3m apart; they are utterly filled with schools of fusiliers and snapper. Brilliant gold and yellow gorgonians jut out from the walls like impenetrable curtains—a spectacular photographic opportunity with a wide-angle lens.

On your way back, take the safe swim-through on the north side of the first sister, which exits to more shallow bommies. Abundant fish and coral can keep your safety stop interesting. You could also keep swimming to the wall on the edge of the back reef to finish off in the shallows.

40 Flynn Reef - Coral Gardens

Flynn Reef has several well-known dive sites including **Gordon's Mooring** and **Tracy's Bommie**, which supply good swim-throughs, walls, overhangs, crevices and night diving. The Coral Gardens mooring sits in 8m on a sandy bottom. In front, a wall stretches from 5m to the surface along the reef edge.

Extending back from the wall are superb coral gardens—staghorns among terraces of table corals, boulder coral heads and plates. Soft corals sway in between. Practice your no-touch diving here. Dropping away from this coral plateau is a terracing slope down 10 to 20m.

This slope is also richly covered in coral and more giant clams. Deeper you will see fan corals and more staghorn thickets on the sand. Clownfish, batfish, trout, cod, fusiliers, butterflyfish and angelfish,

Location: *Atlantic Clipper* mooring

Depth Range: 1-27m (3-90ft)

Access: Boat

Expertise Rating: Novice

basslets and whitetip reef sharks are some of the frequent visitors to this

LEN ZELL

An octopus changes color according to its substrate or mood. Look for it by the tell-tale pile of shells outside its lair.

site. You may see grey reef sharks and octopus, along with more common moray eels, barracuda, lionfish and nudibranchs.

Good pelagic action is common with trevally and mackerel adding to the passing parade in deeper water. Once you turn back to the wall, the many terraces, gullies and mini overhangs provide more critters than you'll have time to see. Wrasse, parrotfish, rabbitfish, anthias and butterflyfish perform unique antics down the slope. Do your safety stop in any of the coral gardens; they are so full of life, you'll want to stay even longer.

41 Upolu Reef - Lugger's Lagoon

This unique lagoon on Upolu Reef so closely resembles the shape of the Mediterranean Sea that Seahorse Sail & Dive staff instruct divers to "sail in through the Straits of Gibraltar, then dive and snorkel the Suez Canal and Depths of Dakar or drift the Casablanca Coast." This area is ideal for introductory dives and snorkeling due to its shallow depths and range of small walls, overhangs, coral patches and fish life.

Giant clams and a great range of hard and soft corals adorn the lagoon. The clams tend to mainly brownish, green and blue; smaller ones tend to be a more iridescent turquoise, blue and green. Identify the staghorn and plate coral colonies by the single polyp at the tip of each branch. Brain and boulder corals are

Location: Seahorse Sail & Dive mooring at Upolu Reef

Depth Range: 1-10m (3-33ft)

Access: Boat

Expertise Rating: Novice

also common. A small whitetip reef shark or turtle may join in your lagoonal explorations. Watch for blue-spotted rays resting with sea cucumbers on the sand.

If you go back out the entrance (the "Straits of Gibraltar"), you'll drop away to 20m. Walls and crevices on either side slope away to a sandy rubble floor. Coral patches cover the lower slopes.

BOB HALSTEAD

Blue-spotted stingrays hang out on the sandy bottom.

Crown-of-Thorns Sea Stars

LEN ZELL

Crown-of-thorns sea stars are magnificent animals, growing up to 80cm (30 inches) in diameter, with up to 20 arms covered in 4cm- (2 inch-) long spines. Each spine is coated with a toxin that is released on contact with human skin. This can be a very painful ordeal, especially if you get spines stuck in your joints.

The crown-of-thorns' spiny skin and internal hydraulic system, which drives hundreds of tube feet in grooves under each arm, lends it enough agility to move around and over almost any coral colony. Once it finds living corals, it turn its bubbly white stomach inside-out, over the living tissue, digesting it off its skeleton. When finished the crown-of-thorns moves on, leaving a round white scar. Usually it feeds at night and hides by day. Small crabs will nip at its tube feet to keep it off branching coral; harlequin shrimp will attack and eat it, as do triton shells and some triggerfish.

Crown-of-thorns have an incredible ability to regenerate from just one severed arm and part of the central disc. This coral-killing beast can aggregate in the millions on one reef while, on another reef, form small chronic populations that slowly kill the coral. Each female can release up to 60 million eggs each breeding season. Egg survival may be enhanced by El Niño, coastal run-off or many unknown factors. Reefs usually recover, sometimes only to be eaten again.

Why so many outbreaks throughout Indo-Pacific reefs? That's the big question that many hypotheses try to address. Linneaus named the crown-of-thorns in the 1700s, although some geologists say that spines found in reef sediments indicate outbreaks more than 5,000 years ago. Recent data collected by scientists and Marine Park staff will slowly shed light on the "hows and whys" of this fascinating creature and its distribution. Since the creature has only been consistently observed in the last 30 years, there is still much to be learned.

42 Michaelmas Reef

Michaelmas Reef is 10km long with a sand cay, which is an important rookery for sooty and crested terns. This site description is an amalgamation of many, but is demonstrative of most dives you will get to do here—this reef has enormous potential for diving.

Location: Northwest reef back

Depth Range: 1-20m (3-66ft)

Access: Boat

Expertise Rating: Novice

Giant clams are the most common delightful feature of this reef. You will see them whether you snorkel the shallows or dive to 20m, although they are more prolific in the shallows. Also look for the soft corals with hard bases that contribute to reef growth throughout.

Walls, swim-throughs, gullies, small caves and overhangs are found in most areas and are often home to whitetip reef sharks. Snorkeling takes you over shallow reeftops riddled with holes, crevices and many giant clams. Smaller burrowing clams are common and tend to be more iridescent and varied in color. Blue-spotted rays and sea cucumbers are common on the sandy floors with schools of damsels and fusiliers all over the corals.

If you walk in the sand near the beach of the cay, you'll have the disconcerting experience of fish, and sometimes small sharks, dashing in and "biting" at your heels. Fear not! They are merely trying to catch the shrimp and other animals that lift up out of the sand as you walk along. These fish have learned that humans are useful for something. The faster or more vigorously you move, the more excited they will become as you'll be stirring up more food for them!

As you explore the bommies, you'll encounter batfish, cleaner stations, nudibranchs, crayfish, turtle weed clumps and a constantly changing parade of life.

Clumped staghorns and soft corals dominate the back reef crest at Michaelmas Reef.

43 Breaking Patches

A giant-stride entry off the boat drops you into 15m to a sandy floor. You'll have several sites to choose from including **The Wall, Peroxide Bommie** or **The Gap.** If you take a dinghy you could dive the **Fish Market** or **North Point Drift.** Regardless of which site you visit, there is a wall, pinnacle, rich coral head, edge or floor waiting for you.

Location: Paradise Reef

Depth Range: 0-20m (0-66ft)

Access: Boat

Expertise Rating: Novice

The sandy floors yield several species of sea cucumbers eating their way around. Two Maori wrasse, pet-named Hamish and Rasmus, are regulars here and appear to like affection from some of the guides. Christmas tree worms, giant clams and sometimes anemones reward careful observers. Clownfish, basslets, damsels and butterflyfish are common, and lionfish hang out under overhangs.

Going left from the boat along The Wall keeps you in less than 18m. A spectacular array of soft and hard corals add color to the constant swarm of fish. Plate and fan corals make up the majority of coral life in shallow water.

If you go out to the Fish Market, larger fish like trout, cod, parrotfish and wrasse join pelagics, such as barracuda and tuna. The bommies rise from 25 to 2m—once deep, lie on your back and look up the walls for a buzz. They provide a few swim-throughs and good overhangs with a sand floor rich in staghorn thickets and anemones.

PHIL WOODHEAD

A coral medley covers the mid-reef slope at Breaking Patches.

44 Holmes Reef - Amazing

From the sheer walls and pinnacles, swim-throughs and sandy floors to the abundant life throughout the whole area, this site is truly "amazing"—in its appearance from the surface and as you dive it.

Descend from a giant-stride entry off the boat, which is moored onto a small coral pinnacle and its nearby sandy floor. If the whitetip reef sharks haven't totally distracted you, then you may see the thousands of tiny "umbrella handles" sticking out of the sand, seemingly dancing and disappearing as you approach.

Location: Holmes Reef

Depth Range: 5-40m+ (16-130ft+)

Access: Boat

Expertise Rating: Advanced

These are garden eels and are always seen here. Take your time approaching; you'll seldom get closer than about 4m before they pull into their burrows.

LEN ZELL

Sunbeams and playful streams of light make exploring the caves truly "amazing."

PHIL WOODHEAD

Red bass join whitetip and grey reef sharks as they circle, waiting expectantly for food.

Down the slope at 35m are two large coral outcrops called The Matterhorn because they look like mountains protruding from the snow. These mountains have glorious sea fans, soft corals, fairy basslets and cruising grey reef sharks. Be careful of your depth here as it drops away to 60m.

Back up the slope, the reef starts at 25m rising quickly to 10m. This wall is where the amazing swim-throughs can be found. They all have a laser show of sunbeams streaking through the holes above, so you don't need a light for daytime entries. Watch for the several resident potato cod and spotted sweetlip schools. Banded coral shrimp give themselves away with their long white antennae poking out of the crevices.

As you finish your dive with a safety stop at the top of the mooring pinnacle, you'll be entertained by clownfish, passing bluespot trevally and sometimes giant trevally.

Night diving here is easy due to the shallows and complex of gullies and swim-throughs. If you turn your light toward yourself (so the beam is hidden), you'll see a spectacular display of flashlight fish.

45 Holmes Reef - Nonki

Named by a Japanese diver, this site is easy going and has something for everyone. The mooring is tied to the top of a coral pinnacle, which rises from 36m—the bottom slopes off the edge into the deep blue. You can always see the pinnacle from the boat as you enter the water. A few years ago the top was badly damaged by an anchor chain but is now recovering slowly. Several smaller coral heads are nearby but are too deep for most divers.

After the giant-stride entry off the dive platform, follow the mooring line to the pinnacle and drop down its side to

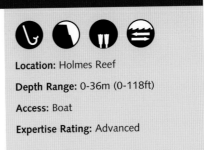

Location: Holmes Reef

Depth Range: 0-36m (0-118ft)

Access: Boat

Expertise Rating: Advanced

your planned depth. Begin spiralling slowly upwards. Schools of bigeye trevally are at the base and top of the pinnacle, often giving you the sensation of being totally surrounded by fish.

Sea fans of many colors jostle for space against red spiky softs and profuse hard corals. Look carefully and you will see nudibranchs, longnose hawkfish, pyramid butterflyfish and juvenile golden snappers. Anemones host several species of clownfish, and usually shy clown triggerfish visit the transparent shrimp cleaner stations on the bubble corals. While in its "being cleaned trance," the trigger's wild coloring can be observed closer than normally possible.

Large dogtooth tuna cruise by in the blue. Divers regularly see grey reef sharks, occasional silvertip sharks and even rare hammerheads. Turtles are also regular visitors and cuttlefish duck in near the coral.

A swim-through crowded with sea fans and soft corals is excellent, but be careful to not damage them. More delights are revealed once you emerge into the shallows for a safety stop. Table corals, small brains and others provide good lookouts for hawkfish and grazing points for parrotfish and rabbitfish. Clouds of fairy basslets and damselfish always are a delight.

PHIL WOODHEAD

Circling bigeye trevally.

46 Hastings Reef - The Fish Bowl

Hastings is a large, popular diving and snorkeling reef, with over 13km of reef edge and back reef sand floors to explore. Upon entering the water from TUSA Dive's mooring at The Fish Bowl, go forward to the wall, which runs along the back edge of the reef and drops to a sandy floor at 8 to 12m.

Location: TUSA Dive mooring

Depth Range: 0-16m (0-53ft)

Access: Boat

Expertise Rating: Novice

Anemones and clumps of staghorn coral are regular features with giant clams perched on the shallow reeftop and bommies. Sweetlip, cod and trout are regulars and schools of damsels are common. Pairs of butterflyfish and angelfish, feeding among the coral, add more splashes of color. The wall winds around and along, bringing you to more clams and a good swim-through up into the reef. After exploring it, go left around the group of bommies. Note the giant clam in 12m on the outer edge of the base.

You can go back the way you came along the wall or take a different depth route out over the floor. Whitetip reef sharks and lagoon rays often rest on the sandy floor.

On some of the coral patches you will see long white tentacles extending out over the sand. These are the feeding

PHIL WOODHEAD

Hastings Reef is an excellent stage for composing terrific wide-angle shots.

threads of a *Terrebellid* worm and if you get very close to the ribbon-like tentacles, you will see lumps of food being carried along inside them. Also notice the daytime coral with its polyps out about 6 to 10cm—if you look around you will often find broken-off satellite pieces establishing new colonies.

47 Saxon Reef

Another popular spot used by several operators, this is an excellent back reef with several night or day dive sites. They are combined here into one "mega site." Snorkeling anywhere on the shallow bommie tops, reef edge and reeftop is excellent.

The reeftop exposes on supreme low tides and a wall drops down to 8m onto a white sand floor. As you move out from the wall, large patches of staghorn coral thickets and small bommies are interspersed with large single- and mixed-species bommies. Swim-throughs and gullies are scattered throughout the area. Your guide will help show you the best sites to explore.

There is no need to go below 18m, as the rubble sand and few coral patches pale into insignificance when compared to the life up the slope. Each bommie has its own special feature and life associated with it—giant clams, anemones, coral-

Location: TUSA Dive & *Atlantic Clipper* moorings

Depth Range: 1-20m (3-66ft)

Access: Boat

Expertise Rating: Novice

limorpharians, pipefish, lionfish and moray eels. Occasionally a turtle will cruise by, as will large cod and the ever-present schools of damsels and fusiliers. Common passing pelagics include tuna, mackerel, trevally and barracuda.

The white sandy floor reflects light and on a sunny day turns the whole area into a classic magical reef scene. Wide-angle photography and macro work well here, but watch the sand glare effect. Giant clams are great subjects. Notice nesting titan triggerfish in summer, as they protect their "bomb crater" nests with crash-tackling effectiveness.

LEN ZELL

Deceptively pretty, lionfish have highly venomous dorsal spines.

JOHN BARNETT

Pipefish are slender versions of their seahorse cousins, feeding on crustaceans at night.

48 Norman Reef - Troppo Lounge

This reef has moorings belonging to several dive operations and each uses different parts of the back of this superb little reef.

Maori wrasse, moray eels, giant clams, anemones and their commensals are permanent features. Along the reef back are a series of large bommies, staghorn thickets and hillocks of rich coral cover. Sandy areas deeper down often have garden eels but you need to wait for them to emerge as they are extremely timid.

Almost all dives start with a giant-stride entry from the boat. You either swim up to the shallows or out deeper and then back in depending on your experience. Amphitheater-like sandy floors are surrounded by coral hillocks, reef edge and bommies. Take your time around the bommies and at the reef edge, as there are some excellent swim-throughs and a few caves, some of which are not safe for divers. You will need a guide to lead the way and show you which ones are safe. Walls of all sizes and shapes with gullies, crevices and over-hangs are common.

In mid- to late winter, minke whales take over this whole area of reefs. Batfish, drummers, spangled emperors, fusiliers and red bass join in.

Look for some of the large, Maori wrasse that hang

Location: TUSA Dive & *Atlantic Clipper* moorings

Depth Range: 0-27m (0-90ft)

Access: Boat

Expertise Rating: Novice

around, particularly if you "ignore" them. Pay them any specific attention and they tend to shy away. Turtles are regulars, but will normally leave as soon as you see them. Moray eels can be found throughout the area, with blue-spotted rays and giant clams common on the sandy floor.

Wide-angle and macrophotography are both rewarding here and occasional whitetip sharks add a thrill as you get the shot.

LEN ZELL

Look for spotted morays in small nooks and crannies.

Underwater Photography & Video

Whether you're shooting classic diver-among-coral scenes, detailed macros or nesting turtles on sand, the GBR offers every conceivable opportunity for great underwater and above water shots. How your images turn out will depend on a lot of variables: the system you use, what kind of film (whether it be photographs, film, video or digital), prevailing weather and water conditions.

Most importantly, know your system well *before* you bring it into the field. Unfortunately, the rule of "the more you pay the better the results" is true for land and underwater photography, assuming also that you know how to properly use your gear. If you want to be a serious underwater photographer, you will need to use a housing for your video or SLR camera, or get the Nikonos system with lights or strobe.

Rental underwater photography equipment is available in a few places, but is often limited in its capacity. If you want to rent gear, contact your dive operator well in advance so they can help you make special arrangements. Another choice is to buy one of the "happy snap" amphibious cameras now available—buy one, use it and enjoy the one or two good pictures you will get. They work to about 4m before the controls go haywire, so they are only good for snorkeling or very shallow diving.

Taking Pictures

Light is the key to photography and underwater photography in the tropics is no exception—glare, turquoise reef waters, deep blue waters, bright sunshine and water filtering colors all add to the challenge. Add choppy surface, backscatter, condensation, currents, waves and you see why underwater photography is so difficult and yet rewarding to those who persist.

If you know what the light is doing underwater you will be successful. Underwater red and other longer wavelengths are filtered out in about the first meter, so you need to reconsider the whole light spectrum to achieve the effects you see in documentaries, magazines and brochures. This can only be done with a strobe or lights. Avoid backscatter by hand-holding your strobe or light as far away as possible—but still in front of your camera—without getting lens flare. Filters are important, polarizing above-water red of varying intensity, according to your video type, film and light system.

LEN ZELL

Wide-angle lenses—such as a 15mm Nikonos or equivalent for a housed SLR with a dome port—are best for underwater scenes. A wider angle lens improves the apparent visibility and lets you make better use of your strobe. Remember, the strobe light goes out 1m to the subject and then back 1m. This means it goes through 2m of water filtering before it exposes, so lots of red is lost even at a 1m distance. For small subjects, the 1:1, 1:2, 1:3 extension tubes for Nikonos or macro lenses for SLRs are best. Follow your handbook instructions carefully, bracket the important shots and hope for lots of good luck.

Caring for Your Camera

Your gear will only perform well if you care for it well—dropping it into a regulator wash bin, throwing it onto the deck, mishandling moveable parts, etc. will eventually lead to a leak. Always wash gear at the end of every dive—at least an hour of soaking is best. Do not use the same setup for consecutive dives without careful checks and servicing. Divers who hug their gear like a long-lost lover will generally not have problems—at least with the gear!

If you are diving from an air-conditioned boat, beware that when you take your camera outside the moisture will fog up your lens. Only take it out in the housing, or take it out in a waterproof case and wait 12 hours for it to warm up. You can also use a dry T-shirt wrapped around the camera in a sealed plastic bag for a fast one-hour warm-up, just be sure not to overheat the film.

Similarly, if you put the unit together in hot, steamy conditions and then go straight into the water, the ports will usually fog up. It's best to set up in air-conditioning if you can, and then consider storing your camera outside, taking it back inside only as required. Another safety feature is to pack several cellulose sponges around the camera (inside the housing) each time you dive—these will soak up any water that gets in, hopefully keeping the camera moisture-free.

Film & Processing

In Australia, film and processing costs are generally higher than those paid overseas, so it's best to buy film before you come. Film and processing are available in all major centers for both slide E6 and color prints. E6 usually takes 24 hours, or faster if you pay more. Kodachrome film has to go to Sydney and takes 7 to 14 days, but includes processing and mounting. Some resorts and boats have one-hour color print services.

Use a neutral color, such as Caucasian skin, to gauge the color you want.

Slide film is best for "true" colors, but if you want the images for an album, print is easier and more flexible. Work with the processing people to get the colors you want. Shoot a subject that everyone knows the color of and use that as a reference—average Caucasian skin colors are good for this.

Video

Consider buying a video cassette sold by the operator as a souvenir of your trip. They are usually exceptional value—you get a superb tape of the area, with you appearing as the star. Make sure, however, that you get the format for your home system—Australia is PAL/SECAM, unlike the U.S. NTSC system, and they are not interchangeable.

If you're shooting your own video, know what white balance setting works best for your unit underwater. Use lights if possible and watch when you use the red filter. A red filter that swings on and off inside the housing is very useful for getting "realistic" colors. Watch these filters though, as they can send some white balance settings into major drifts.

Shoot only short, well-planned shots from a variety of perspectives, rather than the rock-n-rolling seasick-producing long shots of a whole 45 minute dive. Ten minutes of tape from an hour's dive is a lot. Be prepared for no one to take any interest in your results unless the shots are short, steady and interesting.

Photographer's Checklist

Practice with your gear at home in the bath or pool before traveling. Know all the necessary in-field servicing you must do and bring all the support gear you will need:

- grease
- tissues
- film (remember that film is the cheapest part of your holiday, so use lots of it!)
- batteries
- manual
- carrying cases
- insurance
- tools
- chargers
- spare parts
- patience, humor and good luck!

Port Douglas Dive Sites

Once a quiet fishing village accessed by dirt road from the highway, Port Douglas is now a famed hideaway for movie stars and presidents. No longer a sleepy village, it is decidedly casual, tropical and energetic.

Port Douglas is the coastal center closest to both the Wet Tropics of Queensland (an area that includes 19 national parks, 31 state forests, five timber reserves and one Aboriginal reserve) and the GBR. Both areas were designated UNESCO World Heritage sites in 1988 and 1981, respectively.

Its sandy beaches are ideal for strolls and a medley of adventure activities. You can access the reefs from large wave-piercing catamarans through to smaller 10-person vessels. Popular destinations include Low Isles, just 15km offshore. Low Isles have a sand cay and a closed mangrove cay, which are home to thousands of nesting Torresian imperial pigeons from August to February.

Agincourt, Opal and Tongue Reefs are also popular and, as they sit on or close to the outer edge of the continental shelf, visibility is better than inshore reefs. Extended trips to the Ribbon Reefs, Coral Sea and far northern reefs leave from Port Douglas.

Port Douglas Dive Sites	Good Snorkeling	Novice	Intermediate	Advanced
49 Tongue Reef - Turtle Bay	●	●		
50 Opal Reef - Barracuda Pass	●		●	
51 Agincourt Reef - Nursery Bommie	●	●		
52 Bougainville Reef - The Zoo	●		●	
53 Pickersgill Reef & Cay	●	●		
54 East Hope Island	●	●		
55 Ribbon Reef No 3 - Steve's Bommie	●	●		
56 Pixie's Pinnacle	●	●		
57 Snake Pit			●	
58 Ribbon Reef No 10 - The Cod Hole	●		●	
59 No Name Reef	●	●		
60 Lizard Island - Cobia Hole	●		●	
61 Osprey Reef - North Horn	●		●	

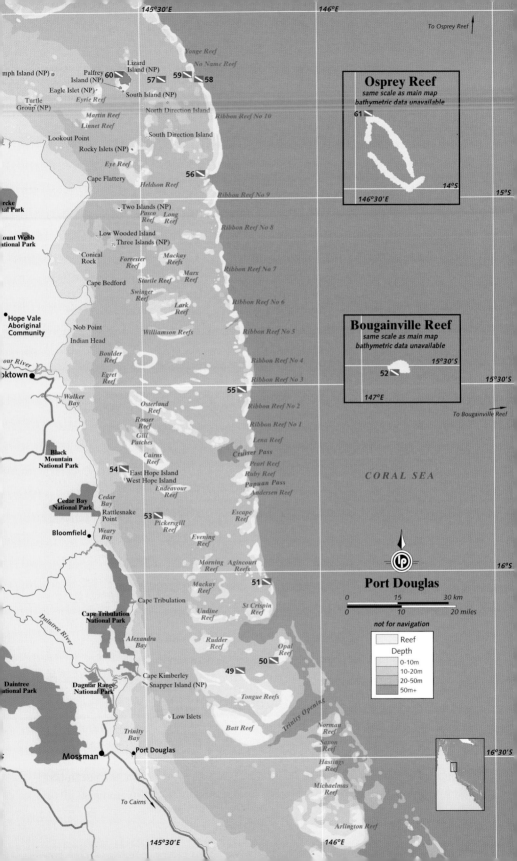

49 Tongue Reef - Turtle Bay

A giant-stride entry puts you face-to-face with Killer, a 35kg Maori wrasse who always expects the divemaster to feed him. He has complete understanding of the situation—you are a diver and you carry pilchards; how he takes them is up to him. Sometimes he is Holly Golitely from *Breakfast at Tiffany's* and other times he becomes Hannibal Lecter from *Silence of the Lambs.*

Location: North end Third Sister Reef in Tongue Complex

Depth Range: 1-15m (3-50ft)

Access: Boat

Expertise Rating: Novice

After the divemaster has negotiated with Killer, you'll find the reef edge in about 3m. Watch for one of several resident turtles. If you are lucky, Dopey, identified by his quiet nature and a nick in his back right flipper, will swim smack into your viewfinder. After a quick pose or two, Dopey says, "I'm out of here," and the cool turtle slowly disappears.

Working along the circle will take you over one enormous giant clam and several species of sea cucumbers on the sandy floor of this back reef cove. A staghorn thicket and patches hide many smaller reef fish, which also tuck in along the small walls and bommies.

A good mixture of soft and hard corals cover the reef edges and small bommies. Check under the plate corals for hovering trout, sweetlip and the occasional barramundi cod.

Finish the dive in the shallows adjacent the reef edge. It is an easy swim back to the boat—the bottom can be interesting for anyone willing to look hard for the small, cryptic life.

50 Opal Reef - Barracuda Pass

Port Douglas dive boat operators love North and South Opal reefs for the numerous great dive sites, including **Bashful Bommie, Ayer's Rock, SNO, Cathedrals, Split Bommie, Blue Buoy,** and **One Fin Bommie**. At Barracuda Pass, your entry drops you into a "sandbox" in 6m, which leads the way to a line of small bommies connected by beautiful coral gardens and sandy floors.

Location: Between south and main Opal Reefs, Poseidon & Haba moorings

Depth Range: 1-15m (3-50ft)

Access: Boat

Expertise Rating: Intermediate

You can also start outside the pass for a drift dive. Either way, use the reef edge for your navigation and watch your buddy and guide for a safe return. The tides bring lots of plankton through this opening, attracting smaller fish, which, in turn, attract bigger fish, and so on.

Note the bottom here—the size of the sand grains gives an idea of how rugged it can get around reefs. Sea cucumbers abound on the sand—look at them carefully for commensals if you can tear your eyes away from the superb soft and hard corals and grazing fish. You may see the occasional lagoon ray in the sand as well. As you hit deeper water on your left, the fish life increases on your right. Schools of paddletails, trevally, mackerel, red bass and three species of barracuda move around slowly. A resident blacktip reef shark may also show itself.

This underwater rolling hills-and-valleys area of coral is interspersed with sand. The nursery plate, which consists of three plate corals about 40cm off the sand, shelters a succession of juvenile whitetip reef sharks—you'll see at least one on any given visit. An occasional giant clam occurs and watch out for titan triggerfish digging their crater-shaped nests—they can get very aggressive in summer. This is a superb site in most conditions and always great for photography.

LEN ZELL

Barracuda cruise by a horse's tooth coral colony.

LEN ZELL

Plate corals grow in thin sheets and shingles, encrusting and overlapping one another.

51 Agincourt Reef - Nursery Bommie

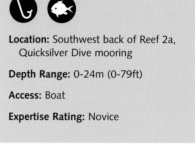

Agincourt Reef is a complex of many smaller reefs, has snorkel sites at the pontoons and at least 16 excellent dive sites, including **Point Break, Three Sisters, Horseshoe Reef** and the **Fish Bowl**.

Pieces of a Taiwanese wreck are featured at **The Wreck**. Giant clams appear at all the sites, along with resident Maori wrasse. You can dive drifts, walls or swim-throughs, and see big fish and turtles. Meander in coral gardens and look for the garden eels found at various locations.

At the Nursery Bommie, a dramatic coral pinnacle rises from 24m with 20m-width at the top. Spiky soft corals grow at the base with more softs and whips as you ascend to 18m, where two giant

Location: Southwest back of Reef 2a, Quicksilver Dive mooring

Depth Range: 0-24m (0-79ft)

Access: Boat

Expertise Rating: Novice

morays, which can be a little aggressive at times, provide some drama. Spiral slowly up and around the bommie.

Huge clouds of fairy basslets and other planktivores hover out in the current. Yellow-striped snapper and schools of barracuda circle the outside edges, always looking for a small fish meal. Lionfish, drummer and unicorn-fish are common, with clownfish and their host anemones in the shallower sections, surrounded by staghorn clumps and boulder corals. A photographer's delight, this site offers myriad opportunities to get the classic reef shot. Macros are also good, with small life in the many micro overhangs and shrimp in anemones and long-tentacle mushroom corals.

CRAIG LAMOTTE

Aerial oblique of Agincourt Reefs.

52 Bougainville Reef - The Zoo

As one of the smaller Coral Sea Reefs, Bougainville has a delightful array of dive sites, ranging from moorings to drifts. **The Sticks** and **Between Wrecks** are great drifts, while **Deep Six, Dungeons & Dragons, West Point, The Junkyard** and **Corner Shop** are all accessed from moorings or hot boats. These sites present a challenge for photographers; the diversity

Location: Mike Ball's *Spoilsport* anchorage

Depth Range: 5-40m+ (16-130ft+)

Access: Boat

Expertise Rating: Intermediate

of life is so dramatic here, you'll be faced with the taxing dilemma of whether to take your wide-angle or macro lens. Good luck with your decision! (Hint: On a clear day, go wide.)

At The Zoo, follow the mooring line down to the large coral bommie then go to the coral sand gully or onto the outside wall. Either direction will be rewarding.

The sand gully slopes down from 14 to 30m and is usually a resting place for whitetip reef sharks and sometimes a black cowtail ray. The gully edges supply rich surfaces of coral, algae and coralline algae. There are great spots to find nudi-branchs, flatworms and leopard blennies.

Leading away from the edges of the gully and the shallows of the wall, numerous channels form a labyrinth of swim-throughs. This maze provides all sorts of shady and protected nooks for an array of fish. Surgeonfish, snappers, sweetlips, drummers and many grazers are some of the larger species, while numerous smaller species reward the careful observer.

On the outside wall at 30m, displays of small sea fans and soft corals bloom, with basslets and chromis swarming like bees around flowers. Grey reef sharks patrol the whole area—a great thrill when you meet one coming through a channel.

As you ascend for your safety stop, you will move into the richer coral to marvel at the shallow fish life on the outer edge of the wall. Lucky observers may see rare flame angelfish—once you see one, you'll never forget it.

With cruising green and hawksbill turtles, sharks and general abundance, The Zoo is an appropriate name for this site. Each dive yields new species, which is remarkable in such a confined area.

PHIL WOODHEAD

Flame angelfish are rare and very timid.

Dungeons & Dragons is a maze of caves.

53 Pickersgill Reef & Cay

Primarily used as a snorkel site, this spot is excellent for keen macrophotographers and snorkelers. The boat drops you on the cay's sandy beach, which submerges on big tides. You can venture out in the shallows between coral heads and clams or, if diving, continue over the reef edge.

Location: *Big Mama* anchorage at northwest corner

Depth Range: 1-5m (3-16ft)

Access: Boat to island, entry from beach

Expertise Rating: Novice

The bommies are all sizes and each one is rich with a different suite of animals and plants. Look for large colonies of soft corals in nearer the island—notice some of their bases are hard, made up of the calcium carbonate spines the soft corals secrete. They are major contributors to back reef growth in the northern GBR.

Giant clams provide superb color as their inhalant and exhalant siphons allow you to look inside at their inner workings. They have small light-sensitive cells in their mantles and may sense your shadow as you swim over them, causing them to jerk closed. Christmas tree worms, found in the boulder coral colonies, display a similar closing-up reaction.

Turtles are more common than at sites farther offshore, as the grazing conditions are generally better. In summer, you may see mating pairs or females waiting around to nest on nearby cays. Anemones and their commensal shrimps add interest. Look for clownfish eggs under the anemones. Butterflyfish, surgeons and sometimes a large Maori wrasse will cruise in to check you out.

Over the edge, the sand slopes down quickly and the coral heads provide good animal and plant life. This is a great spot for patient observers.

LEN ZELL

A snorkeler checks out the inner workings of a giant clam.

54 East Hope Island

A giant-stride entry from the boat or a walk out from the beach, puts you into a sandy channel between coral walls that heads down to about 10m. By swimming along the channel to the east, and then turning southeast, you can work your way along the southeast face of the reef. Visibility is usually poor here but the diversity of life makes it a fabulous area for those who take time to look.

Location: Northwest of sand cay

Depth Range: 1-10m (3-33ft)

Access: Boat or beach from island

Expertise Rating: Novice

If you are snorkeling and there is enough water over the reef, turn right over the reeftop and return over it on your way back to the boat. This will let you see tremendous numbers of sea cucumbers, clown triggerfish, algae and fabulous soft corals. Don't pick up cone shells as they can inject you with their fatal dart. Turtles will often graze this area and dugong were reported here in the past.

The Hope Islands offer a great diversity of land and reef species due to the mixture of sandy, muddy and nearshore habitats. West Hope Island is a mangrove on coral shingle and rubble, whereas East Hope Island has rainforest vegetation on sand and is subject to drought. The island is superb for island walking with beautiful vegetation, ospreys and the gentle cooing of Torresian imperial pigeons (in summer only).

Giant clams are scattered throughout and grazing wrasse and parrotfish are especially common. Coral colonies can be enormous, especially the giant boulder coral heads with surrounding plates and stags on the reef edges. Robust staghorns are common and are major contributors to the sand and rubble that make up the reeftop cays.

Look carefully at the sand for high proportions of single-celled forams, which supply a lot of the sand for islands in these areas. Big blue *Linckia* sea stars are common, as are many smaller species of stars, feather stars and the occasional crown-of-thorns.

JOHN BARNETT

Blue sea stars graze on algae and detritus. They have natural suncreen protection that enables them to lounge in shallow waters.

55 Ribbon Reef No 3 - Steve's Bommie

Entry from either the boat or tender drops you into 33m, only meters away from Steve's Bommie, a coral pinnacle that is a real favorite with crew and passengers. Large groups put in sequentially, so they can drop to their planned depth and then spiral up. It is a great site for both introductory dive courses and experienced divers, with a huge selection of marine life—a classic "oasis-in-the-desert" site.

Location: Due west of south end of reef

Depth Range: 3-35m (9-115ft)

Access: Boat

Expertise Rating: Novice

Plate corals, boulder corals, gorgonian fans, soft corals and golf ball corals are all over this place. Nudibranchs are regularly seen, especially below 10m. This is a site where the brochure-like statement, "you'll see circling pods of minke whales, barracuda, giant trevally, baitfish and snapper" can be accurate. It is not common but happens at the right times, usually June to August.

Visibility is usually good, with large, concentrated fish schools and prolific small life. It is a great site for wide-angle or macrophotography and is a popular night dive.

Look for the five species of anemonefish, purple and gold anthias, fourlined snapper and yellowtail goatfish. Chevron barracuda, trevally and whitetip reef sharks regularly cruise by.

Typical clouds of reef fish swirl around Steve's Bommie.

56 Pixie's Pinnacle

Pixie's Pinnacle has the best of everything the GBR has to offer. This site can be done in five minutes or, by slowing down and looking, you can take your time seeing examples of almost every group of organism found on the GBR.

Location: Northwest corner, small plug reef between Ribbons No 9 & 10

Depth Range: 1-27m (3-90ft)

Access: Boat

Expertise Rating: Novice

This coral pinnacle rises from 40m to the surface, where it is about 15m across. By following a slowly descending spiral you will see plenty; finish the dive with an ascending spiral and safety stop.

Hard coral diversity is high at this site, with many small colonies striving to fight their way out from under the larger, faster-growing species. At about 20m a talus (rubble) slope descends on all sides and is decorated with more soft corals. This is a good spot to look for occasional black coral colonies. The talus slope then drops off slowly at varying angles to a 30m bottom. This is often a resting spot for large cod, feeding sea cucumbers, rays and whitetips.

Above the talus slope is a series of vertical walls, overhangs and multitudes of small caves. All provide great hangouts for lionfish, moray eels, shrimp, anemones and their clownfish, cleaner wrasse and hanging spiky soft corals, gorgonians, yellow turret coral, lace corals, sponges, hydroids and molluscs.

ANDY SKIMMING

Swift clusters of anthias flit about the edge of Pixie's.

Fairy basslets create an amazing pink cloud while they feed in the current that bathes the pinnacle. Many animals are well camouflaged, such as the resident stonefish, so patient and observant divers will be rewarded. Be prepared to shoot all your film, with medium- to close-up your best camera lens choice.

Those who can tear their eyes away from the life on the pinnacle, will see the shoals of fish regularly cruising by or hovering off the pinnacle. Fusiliers are common, with trevally, barracuda, mackerel, sharks, batfish and the occasional ray providing a charismatic megafaunal experience.

57 Snake Pit

If you think the skipper is crazy when you stop in the middle of the ocean and he says, "Dive here in the Snake Pit"— you are probably right. Sea snakes are regularly seen at this dive site, which seems like it's in the middle of nowhere.

You drop down onto a submerged series of eight bommies that are roughly aligned in two lines. The northeast line comes to 5m and the southwest to 14m from a 16m sandy bottom. If you swim a few meters away from the bommies to the south or west you could get to 30m quickly.

Location: Halfway between Lizard Island and Ribbon No 10

Depth Range: 5-30m (16-98ft)

Access: Boat

Expertise Rating: Intermediate

Schools of bannerfish and occasional barracuda swarm around you. Check out the manta cleaning station on the northern-most bommie. Look for blue-spotted rays, black-blotched rays and triggerfish on the sandy areas. Olive sea snakes are the regulars here—as always, treat them with respect and let them do their own thing. You may see green and hawksbill turtles. Beautiful pelagic triggerfish move around, their dorsal and anal fins looking like a bolero dancer's cape.

Whips, fans and soft corals abound with diverse and healthy hard corals. Sometimes you will see slatey bream and lionfish hovering down around in the whips or at the bases of coral heads. Nudibranchs, sea stars, feather stars and sea cucumbers are common, and it is a great macro to mid-range lens site.

Give sea snakes, like Slim here, plenty of room to move.

58 Ribbon Reef No 10 - The Cod Hole

Internationally recognized underwater photographers Ron and Valerie Taylor were the first to publicize this fantastic site and were instrumental in its declaration as a protected marine park area in the 1970s. Large potato cod (numbers reported from six to 30) are friendly, especially since they have been regularly fed for over 20 years. Over time the health of the cod has decreased, with cankers and skin disease becoming evident. Their illness is possibly due to the poor food types they were fed, combined with handling by divers.

Location: North end of Ribbon No 10

Depth Range: 10-22m (33-72ft)

Access: Boat

Expertise Rating: Intermediate

Fish feeds are still being done here, but let the divemaster or guide handle the feeding and follow instructions carefully. You dive right off the boat into a cloud of waiting cod, large Maori wrasse, red bass, emperor and many other species, assuming they haven't all been fed by the previous boat. If they have, you may only get the stragglers.

You drop to the sandy floor areas between the bommies, which provide amphitheater-like viewing to watch the fish feeding. The 150kg cod and wrasse will often rush right into the feeding bucket and suck or bite out the contents. They all come close and are superb wide-angle subjects even if they haven't been fed.

Large moray eels did frequent the site but most were removed in the mid-'90s when a divemaster lost her arm after being bitten several times. Morays are like all fed animals: things are fine at first, but when the animals grow to expect food, often losing their ability to forage on their own, they become aggressive if you take the food away. Cod will mouth and bite sometimes but their thousands of small fine teeth cause only minor lacerations.

Other marine life includes average coral cover, anemones, whitetip reef sharks, giant clams, schools of pyramid butterflyfish, Solomon's sweetlip, cleaning stations and feather stars. At the start of the dive, make sure you know what the bottom of your boat looks like, so you can return to the right one. If you hear boat engines, watch carefully for propellers above.

LEN ZELL

Potato cod can weigh up to 150kg (330lbs). Decades of hand-feeding by divers (and their sunscreen-coated hands) has taken a toll on these huge fish.

Fish Feeding

The GBRMPA defines fish feeding as "the deliberate attraction of fish... to allow tourists to view them." Many operators feed fish for semi-submersible, platform, snorkel or scuba viewers.

In the past, reasonable concern was expressed about fish feeding because some people were using garbage. Human foods are not suitable for fish as they normally eat a range of unprocessed foods. Feeding can change fish behavior; encouraging them to falsely rely on an unreliable food source, which may cause aggressive behavior, especially if the food source suddenly becomes unavailable.

Only one fish feeding station is allowed at any one site and fish cannot be hand-fed. The food must be fresh, raw marine products or commercially available and approved aquaculture food. No more than 1kg per day can be released and only staff can do the feeding.

59 No Name Reef

The backs of all the Ribbon Reefs have beautiful sandy floors that slope down to the continental shelf floor at 30 to 40m. They often have deep channel walls on their south and north ends, ground in by strong currents on big tide runs. This site has a large bommie adjacent to the inside end of the reef. Divers can have an

Location: Due west of south end of reef

Depth Range: 1-40m (3-130ft)

Access: Boat

Expertise Rating: Novice

easy lagoonal type dive in 10 to 16m, or they can choose to go outside to the west and south, around the bommie where the wall drops away to 40m.

The sandy floor is rich with staghorn corals, while other hard and soft coral communities grow on the walls, reef edges and bommie. Daisy, a 1m-long estuary cod, is a regular in the shallows. Whitetip reef sharks can appear anywhere around here. Lizardfish perch on the

Yellow damselfish hover over their eggs.

corals but rush off when approached, as do feeding goatfish, with their barbels tickling food out of the sand.

Outside on the wall a great display of basslets and fusiliers hover for plankton brought in by the tide. You'll also see schools of pelagic barracuda, mackerel and trevally. Small yellow damsels often flutter around soft coral fans in summer, to protect the eggs they've laid on a dead part of the coral colony. Cleaner wrasse maintain stations in many shallower areas with red bass and sweetlip being good customers. Stinging hydroids and pink lace corals are seen in the overhangs and gullies are rich in coral cover and fish. Beware the tide run on the outside and plan your dive well.

60 Lizard Island - Cobia Hole

Lizard Island is home to an exclusive resort with an airstrip and a research station. Camping is allowed with a permit from National Parks.

Your descent at the Cobia Hole takes you onto a submerged mooring float that usually has circling pelagic barracuda or trevally. The cobia have not been seen regularly for years, but watch for them off the rocks or on the sandy bottom at 14m. There you'll come across a pinnacle of rocks covered with every conceivable group of marine organism.

Macrophotographers will delight in this area. The sponges, soft corals, coralliamorpharians, feather stars, sea stars, sea squirts and their commensal shrimps, crabs and gobies could occupy you all day. This is described as another veneer community, where the reef covers the island rock and fish life moves in and occupies the site. Sea whips, gorgonian fans and stinging hydroids with hovering slaty bream can often be seen. The numerous nooks and crannies guarantee a con-

Location: Off point, northeast of Watson's Bay

Depth Range: 14-18m (46-59ft)

Access: Boat

Expertise Rating: Intermediate

stant supply of interesting sponges, lace corals and sea squirts.

Often large turtles, toadfish and estuary cod will appear here as well. If

LEN ZELL

Feather stars and green coral trees reach out to the nutrient-rich current.

LEN ZELL

A peanut worm lives inside each solitary peanut coral and drags it around with its proboscis.

by some remote chance you run out of subjects on the rocky areas, try looking out on the sea grasses and algae on the nearby sand—make sure your buddy comes and the guide knows where you went.

There are many other good dives around the island, including the inner lagoon. Snorkeling is popular wherever you can get into the water.

61 Osprey Reef - North Horn

Osprey has many sites and the entrances provide several good spots for overnight anchorages and moorings. The North Horn site is best known for its resident population of whitetip reef sharks.

This site has been used for shark feeding for more than 15 years, so the silvertip and grey reef sharks, potato cod, morays and many smaller species are familiar with humans as an irregular feeding source. With assistance from the *Undersea Explorer,* the sharks are now under study. Each shark has been identified and is periodically monitored.

Two moorings allow the boat to hang in the safest spot and you dive off into water that drops to almost 1,000m. The reef edge is an easy 20m swim away. Divers gather at 16 to 20m and, when all is set, the food is brought down and the action begins. The bolder whitetips come in, followed by potato cod. Gradually grey reef sharks build up the courage to start feeding and they are closely followed by silvertips. A 45kg dogtooth tuna disappeared in under two minutes once, so if you want a photograph you have to be quick.

Follow the divemaster's instructions as he or she best knows the behavior of these species. Schooling scalloped hammer-

Location: *Undersea Explorer* mooring at northwest tip of reef

Depth Range: 2-20m+ (6-66ft+)

Access: Boat

Expertise Rating: Intermediate

heads and great hammerheads, seen here seasonally when the waters cool, always bring a quiet awe over divers.

If you have the time, experience and air, explore the big soft-coral trees deeper down on the western wall. You will always see great pelagic action including three-spot dart, dogtooth tuna, rainbow runners and mackerel, feeding on the stunning planktonic animals that float by. Snorkeling over the whole wall and nearby reeftop with its gullies, stinging coral and fish life is also a buzz.

Diving the nearby sites at night will let you see flashlight fish, pelagic octopus, pleurobranchs, crabs, shrimps and sleeping fish. As part of its many diving and research expeditions, the *Undersea Explorer* will trap a nautilus, take its details and then release it, allowing you to observe and swim with it.

PHILLIPE GUIGUEL

Shark-feeding is only possible on Coral Sea reefs and is prohibited within the GBRMP boundaries.

Far Northern Reefs Dive Sites

As this area is 370 to 930km (200 to 500 nautical miles) north of Cairns and Port Douglas, no diving services have set itineraries to these remote reefs. The area includes all the reefs and islands from Lizard Island to the tip of Cape York. Several boats make annual expeditions and others run charter trips on an "as required" basis. These reefs are accessible via Cairns and Port Douglas, or you can fly into Lizard Island, Iron Range or Thursday Island.

LEN ZELL
Following the coral wall.

About 600 reefs, ranging in size from a few meters across to 35km (22 miles) long and 15km (9 miles) wide, provide thousands of diveable reef edges, and that's not including the floors, lagoons and shoals in between the reefs. Included in the Far Northern Reefs is the largest single Marine National Park zone of the GBR Marine Park, covering approximately 2,700 sq nautical miles (9,750 sq km).

More than one hundred cays and many mainland islands also provide stunning terrestrial habitats. Many are closed or permit-only due to their status as Aboriginal sites, or as bird and turtle rookeries. Raine Island, which once had over 16,000 green turtles nesting in one night, is an important rookery for frigate birds, Nankeen night herons, gannets and terns. It is closed at all times.

The best reefs for diving are on the outer edges of the continental shelf from Lizard Island north, adjacent to Cape York. This continuous line of ribbon, deltaic and dissected linear (east-west across the shelf) reefs offer incredible visibility. As this

Far Northern Reefs Dive Sites	Good Snorkeling	Novice	Intermediate	Advanced
62 Tijou Reef - Mr. Walker's Caves	●			●
63 Bligh Boat Entrance	●		●	
64 Mantis Reef	●		●	
65 Great Detached Reef	●		●	●

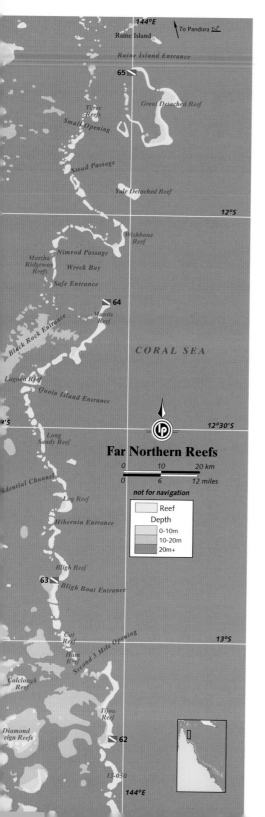

Far Northern Reefs

0   10   20 km

0   6   12 miles

not for navigation

Reef
Depth
0-10m
10-20m
20m+

edge is from 60 to 160km (37 to 99 miles) from the coast, it escapes the coastal run-off that sometimes plagues inshore reefs. Up in the Cape York area, however, outflows from the Fly River in Papua New Guinea wash down in big floods.

As you get closer to the coast there are more islands, less visibility, saltwater crocodiles, tiger sharks and generally less desirable diving conditions.

Moving farther north, toward the center of greatest Indo-Pacific species diversity, it is possible to see not-yet-identified species of corals, fish and other life. In terms of biodiversity, these reefs are the richest of the GBR. Although remote, these areas have been subjected to harvesting for bêche-de-mer, pearl, trochus, and fishing for coral trout, mud crab and barramundi. There are now large no-trawling areas, which help preserve this area.

As boats usually only visit in the summer months during the monsoonal calms, weather permits you to dive any part of the reefs, including the reef front walls and terraces, which are usually smashed by heavy waves. Your boat operator will take you to the easiest and best-suited sites for your ability. Drift dives are often the best way to go.

Wreck Bay, Great Detached Reef, Raine Island and Pandora Entrance are well known for their manta rays, green turtles, whale sharks, sperm whales, Bryde's whales and general pelagic action. There are incredible coral heads, staghorn thickets, cascading algal beds, sand falls and giant clams. You can experience almost every conceivable reef feature, along with historical shipwrecks.

62 Tijou Reef - Mr. Walker's Caves

This continuous series of caves was discovered in 1995 and appears in a mile-long vertical wall from 20 to 35m. They were named in memory of Terry Walker, a great reefie and dive buddy who lost his life in a boating accident in the Gulf of Carpentaria.

The caves extend along the entire west side of a 40m-deep lagoon on the southern end of Tijou Reef, a 24km-long ribbon reef. The whole reef is superb for snorkeling and diving, especially the northern tip at **Shark Point**.

The only access to the lagoons and caves is over the reeftop. If the boat anchors on the west side, numerous small coral heads and patches provide excellent snorkeling in 1 to 5m. This route becomes an exciting drift during tide runs. If the boat anchors on the outside, the reef shelf is also excellent for snorkeling.

The lagoon is unusual because of both depth and the caves, most of which you

Location: West wall of southern lagoon

Depth Range: 1-40m (3-130ft)

Access: Boat

Expertise Rating: Advanced

can enter, although some are quite complex and need ropes. Only experienced cave divers should attempt entry.

Fundraising continues to pay for further research into the cave sediment to determine if there is a break in layers between the terrestrial sediments of the last ice age, and an overlay of marine sediments since resubmergence.

The western lagoon wall is vertical with numerous gullies and overhangs. A sand and rubble slope at its base leads onto a sandy floor. On the east side of the lagoon, a larger sand slope extends from 1 to 5m to the floor. Two large bommies, which are rich in coral and fish, provide good diving and snorkeling.

Large numbers of sharks have been observed here in late November. Their odd and highly aggressive behavior possibly due to breeding. Normally just a few grey reef sharks appear on each dive. Trevally, barracuda and numerous reef species travel along the wall. Triggerfish are common, especially on the sandy floors.

LEN ZELL

Deep sediment covers the floor of Mr. Walker's caves.

63 Bligh Boat Entrance

On the northern tip of reef 12-127, due south of Bligh Reef, is the entrance that Captain Bligh used in his long boat from the *Bounty*. Bligh, along with 18 shipmates, sailed the boat from Tonga to Timor in a 6,874km-long epic journey. Little did they know that only 200 years later, that this would become one of the premier dive sites in the region!

This site is best dived as a drift on an incoming tide. You enter at the notch about a third of the way in and drop to your planned depth. Then go with the flow but be careful, as it is very easy to go deep here. You end the dive at the reef point by popping around the corner and doing a safety stop in the shallows, where the coral is excellent.

On the wall, photographers can shoot wide-angle and enjoy the enormous plate and staghorn corals, gorgonian fans, silvertip and grey reef sharks and barracuda that cruise through here.

Location: Wall along south side of channel

Depth Range: 1-27m (3-90ft)

Access: Boat

Expertise Rating: Intermediate

Alternately, you could go macro to capture the great diversity of small life. Feather stars hang out in the current, sweeping for food. Huge swirling schools of basslets, parrotfish, wrasse, surgeonfish and damsels are almost disorienting. Large soft corals, whips and black tree coral colonies are common.

As the wall is so sharp, it has small gutters near the surface, where sand and algal cascades fall in between the corals and small gully floors. Look for resting whitetip or tawny sharks.

LEN ZELL

Feather stars have tiny hairs called cilia on their arms to carry captured food into their mouths.

64 Mantis Reef

This end of Mantis Reef is spectacular from outside the northern tip to inside along the back edge. Vertical walls, terraces, caves, overhangs, sandy gullies, sand ledges with garden eels and triggerfish nests and shallow bommies add up to excellent diving at many sites.

Outside, on the front, a vertical face stretches almost all along the 19km of reef. This is where you see more great pelagic action with barracuda schools,

Location: Northwest end of Mantis Reef

Depth Range: 1-40m+ (3-130ft+)

Access: Boat

Expertise Rating: Intermediate

LEN ZELL

trevally and fusiliers. Sperm whales and whale sharks have been seen here. Potato cod and gropers are resident and, deeper down, enormous gorgonian fans and spiky soft corals reach out into the waters. Keep an eye out for manta and mobula rays.

If you are snorkeling, the sandy flat area around the shallow bommies at the reef back is a superb coral garden. Butterflyfish, damsels, angelfish, triggerfish and flutemouths are easily seen. Cod, trout and surgeonfish are common, especially in among the staghorn and plate corals.

Due to the remoteness of the site, depths and currents, it is important that you plan your dive and dive your plan well. It is worth it!

Delicate gorgonian fans grow at the base of the wall at Mantis Reef.

65 Great Detached Reef

Great Detached Reef is a large complex of several reefs on an older fossil surface. There are numerous reported shipwrecks on the reeftop—many known and many still unknown. This reef has about 46km of edge, so the dive sites are innumerable. The northwest site is representative of all sites and convenient for anchorage.

Location: Northwest reef, western edge

Depth Range: 2-40m+ (7-130ft+)

Access: Boat

Expertise Rating: Intermediate or Advanced

From the boat, you can go to either side of a small promontory that extends westward from the reef. The reeftop is at 2m and two swim-throughs allow you to cross from side to side. One is closed over the top but easily traversed. Closer to the back edge of the main reef are giant clams and coral gardens in about 8m.

On either side of the ridge is an almost vertical wall that drops away into 200m. Superb pelagics, including barracuda, trevally and sharks, cruise by constantly, along with schools of basslets, fusiliers and sometimes blue-lined snapper.

Soft spiky coral, gorgonians and feather stars add to the color. Stinging coral is common, so be careful. Watch your depths and stick close to the walls for orientation.

JOHN BARNETT

Robust wave-washed corals on the reef crest.

LEN ZELL

Back reef shallows provide calm water for these branching and plate staghorns.

HMS *Pandora*

Culturally significant, the wreck of HMS *Pandora* is one of the oldest known wrecks off Australia's east coast. The ship is best known as the Royal Navy frigate the British Admiralty sent to pursue *Bounty* mutineers. After nearly five months in the South Pacific, the *Pandora* was on her way home with 14 prisoners—mutineers captured in Tahiti, who were locked in a makeshift cell, "Pandora's Box," on the ship's quarterdeck. While exploring a passage through the GBR, the *Pandora* struck a reef on August 28th, 1791. She sank the next morning in 33m (108ft). Of the 35 people who died, four were *Bounty* mutineers.

HMS *Pandora*

The British Admirality went to great lengths to avenge *Bounty* mutineers by dispatching the 24-gun frigate, HMS *Pandora*.

The ship remains have been extensively investigated on expeditions by Queensland museum staff, other professionals and volunteers. The results of the project are on display in a spectacular Maritime Archaeology gallery at the Museum of Tropical Queensland in Townsville.

The Queensland Museum chose to dedicate so much time to the *Pandora* because of its historical importance and archaeological potential. The wreck is exceptionally well preserved and the fascinating array of recovered artifacts enables the museum to reconstruct what life was like onboard an 18th-century European ship. This ambitious effort—the Pandora Project—is funded by government departments and the Pandora Foundation, established to ensure continued support of this and other exciting maritime archaeological project.

To dive the site you must go with a permitted operator who needs to meet strict requirements. Once at the site, you drop straight down to 33m (108ft). Visibility allowing, you can see the stern anchor and sheathing, the bow anchor and the nearby oven, which are the most obvious features. In between is a hard-to-discern coral-covered cannon, swivel guns, a chain pump and many unidentified concretions. An obelisk on the southeast corner contained two of the three skeletons excavated to date.

The dive enlists your sense of history and imagination of the *Pandora*'s voyage over 200 years ago. The top three-quarters of the wooden hull have been eaten away by teredo worms, leaving the ship filled with *Halimeda* algae sands that sent artifacts sliding down into the hull. Poles and frames allow archaeologists to accurately determine where each excavated artifact came from. Shoals of fish mix with the algae and coral that shroud most of the wreck's remains.

Copper stern sheathing at the wreck site.

Torres Strait Dive Sites

Torres Strait includes the northernmost parts of the GBR. The strait connects the Coral and Arafura seas, has a reasonably high tide range and receives the outflow of Papua New Guinea's Fly River. It has strong currents and sediment-rich waters. The tides are poorly understood, making the area hazardous to shipping. You get here via the airport on Horn Island, which is adjacent to Thursday Island, the primary port and administration center for the area.

Leading into the highest reef diversity systems in the world (the Sunda Sea), Torres Strait is the richest part of the GBR Province and is also the most diverse in terms of island and reef morphology.

This region features large platform reefs up to 28km (17 miles) long over mud and sand bases, with numerous islands of mud, sand and shingle. There are also mainland remnants with fringing reefs and small reefs with sand cays. Many of the islands are inhabited by Torres Strait Islanders, who are of Melanesian descent. Rich sea grass communities, mangroves, soft bottoms and reefs support for the rich fish, dugong and turtle populations.

A long history of pearl, trochus and bêche-de-mer industries illustrates the area's colorful past, as evident in the cemetery on Thursday Island. Diving today is limited; few boats offer services due to the general misconception that diving is undesirable here. The western straits are in shallower muddy waters and are unlikely to ever become popular as recreational dive destinations. The eastern straits, however, provide excellent and unique diving opportunities rich in species diversity, and will likely become more popular as services develop.

Sporadic pulses of deep oceanic water slide in under inshore waters, decreasing visibility and temperature. Common features include sheer walls, slopes, lagoons and channels, especially along the outer southeast edge. Farther west, a scattering of reefs have incredible potential as dive sites. Large sharks, whale sharks, turtles and pelagic fish complement the other life.

LEN ZELL

Fringing reef on Wyer Island in Torres Strait.

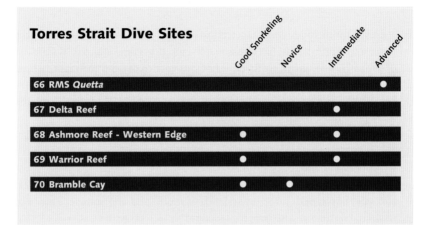

Torres Strait Dive Sites

	Good Snorkeling	Novice	Intermediate	Advanced
66 RMS Quetta				●
67 Delta Reef			●	
68 Ashmore Reef - Western Edge	●		●	
69 Warrior Reef		●	●	
70 Bramble Cay	●	●		

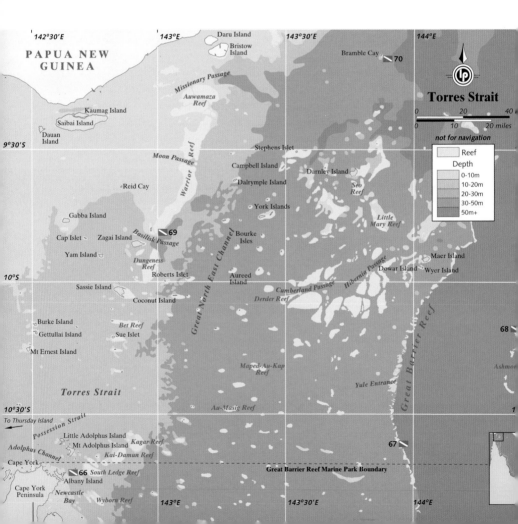

66 RMS *Quetta*

You need a permit to dive this historic site and strong tidal currents make it a difficult dive. You need accurate tide information to hit the 20 minutes of slack water at high or low tide. It is common for divers to be swept away either upon entry or exit on this dive so have your pickup boats and safety sausages sorted out.

Location: East of Cape York on eastern side of Adolphus Channel

Depth Range: 10-24m (33-79ft)

Access: Boat

Expertise Rating: Advanced

You can see the wreck from the surface. Upon descent you'll see a wreck still in reasonably good condition and covered with prolific marine life. Thousands of fish move over, in and around the wreckage.

It would be possible to penetrate many parts of the wreck, but is illegal to do so and certainly no longer safe. The stern lies well exposed, showing the propeller and rudder. Until you reach the enormous gash low on the bow, the ship seems almost intact. Remnants of funnels, masts and other equipment lie scattered around the site. This is a significant wreck, with many items, including the bell, on display at the Quetta Cathedral on Thursday Island.

Sadly, many artifacts were removed prior to its protection as a historic site. Anything you find here should be left alone, photographed if possible, and reported to the Queensland Museum.

The Sinking of the *Quetta*

Like the *Yongala* and the *Gothenberg*, the RMS *Quetta* (1890) was another passenger ship that lost more than one hundred lives. Unlike the others, however, the *Quetta* was not lost during a cyclone, but sunk after striking an uncharted rock off Mt. Adolphus Island, near Cape York. She sank in under three minutes, taking 133 of her 290 passengers and crew with her.

Seasoned wreck divers argue that the *Quetta* is actually a more spectacular wreck dive than the *Yongala*! Access to the *Quetta* is difficult (and expensive), not only because of its remote location,

The *Quetta*'s bell is on display at the Quetta Cathedral.

but mainly because it is exposed to strong currents. All divers should be wary here and it is highly recommended that you dive at slack water.

Unless you have a private vessel, access is easiest by charter dive boat, either from Cairns, Port Douglas or Thursday Island, where a variety of dive charter operators offer extended "dive safari" tours to the far northern GBR.

67　Delta Reef

Scoured by strong currents and rough seas, eaten by crown-of-thorns sea stars, pressured by freshwater run-off from the Fly River, this outer edge reef looks like it has been "hammered" in all ways.

Location: 80km (50 miles) south of Maer Island

Depth Range: 1-35m (3-115ft)

Access: Boat

Expertise Rating: Intermediate

The surface on the outer edge is almost smooth from the wave action slamming into its seaward face. Small deltaic reefs occur between larger outer edge reefs, so it is possible to explore each in one or several dives.

Only species that can grow hard and flat or grooved and strongly encrusted can survive here. Coralline algae and flat, hard corals cover the reef surface. Deeper, the stubby branching and massive colonies become more prominent. As you ascend again, you'll notice some of the same coral species become flatter, reflecting the increased wave action.

On the floor between the reefs is the same scoured calcareous rock seen between the Ribbon Reefs and Pompey Hardlines farther south. Excellent walls appear here with rich cover, although stunted—nothing seems to grow big in these high-energy areas. Life under overhangs and in crevices includes nudibranchs, hydroids, anemones, coralliamorpharians, lace corals, sponges and sea squirts.

Sharks and large pelagic fish are common and curious, with red bass, trout and cod in patchy distributions. Small species, including damsels, basslets and fusiliers are also patchy with wobbegong sharks regularly appearing in the deeper areas.

These small sac-like animals are sea squirts whose larvae have a simple backbone-like structure.

68 | Ashmore Reef - Western Edge

The Western Edge is an outer slope connected by a channel to the lagoon interior. Rich staghorn corals group with big branching blue and brown colonies and many table growth forms. This richness extends to 30m, where the species change from the staghorn group to big fleshy polyp forms and hat corals up to 1m across. The walls have rubble slope bases and rich growths of hard and soft corals.

Location: Western edge of complex

Depth Range: 1-27m (3-90ft)

Access: Boat

Expertise Rating: Intermediate

Large silvertips, grey reef and whitetip reef sharks are common and inquisitive but leave quickly if you command attention. Large pelagic species of mackerel, blue trevally, barracuda and tuna are common, along with fusiliers, damsels, wrasse and parrotfish. Basslets and other open ocean species are common with garden eels poking their heads up out of the sand ledges.

This is good wide-angle photography, although sometimes pulses of dirty water push you to macro systems. Several species of sea snakes are inquisitive but safer if left alone. There are ample shallow coral areas for safety stops and snorkeling.

Trevally cruise through planktiverous fish.

LEN ZELL
A yellow flutemouth swims by coral-covered slope.

69 Warrior Reef

This style of diving is not for the average diver. It is an easy dive, but with muck diving conditions, including low visibility. Combine that with reportings of large tiger sharks, sea snakes, saltwater crocodiles and currents. All these attributes at one dive site can make for interesting and sometimes terrifying times.

These reefs are on a shallow sea floor that is rich in sediment and algae due to currents between the Coral and Arafura seas and the outflow of Papua New Guinea's Fly River. The cays on some of the reeftops are a mixture of rubble, sand and mud and support tall, rich mangrove communities.

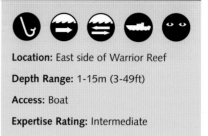

Location: East side of Warrior Reef

Depth Range: 1-15m (3-49ft)

Access: Boat

Expertise Rating: Intermediate

You descend a gentle slope where hard corals are interspersed among large crops of algae, whip corals, soft coral colonies and mangrove leaves. Sea cucumbers are common and you'll find sea urchins in many nooks, also stinging corals with feather stars perched high for food. Look carefully for the tell-tale rippled opening of the famed black-lipped and gold-lipped pearl oysters, harvested for their shells and pearls. Grazing trochus shells are also common in less harvested areas—they are used primarily for buttons.

Large mackerel and whale sharks are almost always seen with rays, hammerhead sharks, tawny sharks and barracuda. Rabbitfish and wrasse are common, along with grazing parrotfish. Painted crayfish are abundant and commonly harvested, but keep an eye over your shoulder if their tails start flapping and they make distress sounds—it's said they are a tiger shark delicacy!

JOHN BARNETT

A hammerhead shark swims by.

70 Bramble Cay

Bramble Cay, identifiable by its light tower, is the northernmost reef of the GBR. It has a sand cay, which has low vegetation. The cay is an important nesting rookery for green turtles.

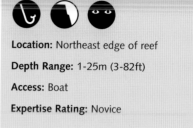

Location: Northeast edge of reef

Depth Range: 1-25m (3-82ft)

Access: Boat

Expertise Rating: Novice

Many dive site possibilities exist around the reef. The southeast side drops down to sand flats at 12 to 30m with some walls, lots of rubble slopes and sediment-resistant coral species. The diversity of coral is high but the coverage is only 5 to 10%. The low visibility makes it more of a macrophotography site.

Balls of boulder corals are alive on every surface. Their shape indicates that they are rolled around by strong waves and currents. The rubble slopes have many encrusting colonies of lettuce corals with free-living species of mushrooms and their cousins. On the wall sections, which drop from 3 to 10m, there are many boulder, elephant skin and soft corals. Whip and gorgonian corals are common. As the area is rich in algae, there are many grazing fish, especially rabbitfish and wrasse with trumpetfish, unicornfish and surgeons equally abundant.

Rabbitfish are algal grazers common in lagoons.

Thousands of green turtles nest on coral cays each year.

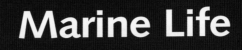

Marine Life

ANDY SKIMMING

The GBR is one of the few places you can see representatives from almost every animal group on the planet—and many you won't see anywhere else. One of the greatest challenges for both scientists and divers lies in trying to identify and name all of these animals.

Common names are used freely but are notoriously inaccurate or inconsistent, and are often subject to geographic colloquialisms. The system that biologists use to differentiate one critter from another is much more accurate. This system is known as binomial nomenclature—the method of using two words (shown in italics) to identify an organism. The first italic word is the *genus*, into which members of similar species are grouped. The second word, the *species*, is the finest detail name and refers to organisms that are sexually compatible and can produce fertile offspring. Where the species or genus is unknown, the naming goes to the next known (and less specific) level: family (F), followed by order (O), class (Cl) and phylum (Ph).

The vertebrates (animals with backbones) and invertebrates (animals without backbones) pictured below are some of the more common critters you'll find in GBR waters.

Common Vertebrates

whale shark
Rhincodon typus

leopard shark
Stegostoma fasciatum

whitetip reef shark
Triaenodon obesus

grey reef shark
Carcharhinus amblyrhyncos

scalloped hammerhead shark
Sphyrna lewini

tassled wobbegong
Eucrossorhinus dasypogon

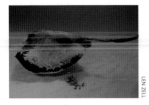

stingray
Taeniura spp.

manta ray
Manta birostris

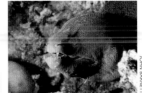

giant moray
Gymnothorax javanicus

variegated lizardfish
Synodus variegatus

flounder
Samariscus triocellatus

trumpetfish
Aulostomus chinensis

spotfin lionfish
Pterois antennata

potato cod
Epinephelus tukula

coral trout
Plectropomus spp.

sweetlip emperor
Lethrinus miniatus

yellowfin goatfish
Mulloidichthys vanicolensis

longfin bannerfish
Heniochus acuminatus

beaked coralfish
Chelmon rostratus

semicircle angelfish
Pomacanthus semicirculatus

flame angelfish
Centropyge loriculus

pink anemonefish
Amphiprion perideraion

green moon wrasse
Thalassoma lunare

hump-headed Maori wrasse
Cheilinus undulatus

parrotfish
F. *Scaridae*

clown triggerfish
Balistoides conspicillum

black-spotted puffer
Arothon nigropunctatus

Common Invertebrates

tube sponge
Ph. *Porifera*

flatworm
Pseudoceros bimarginatus

feather duster worm
Protula sp.

Christmas tree worm
Spirobranchus giganteus

turret coral
Tubastraea sp.

comb gorgonian
Ctenocella pectinata

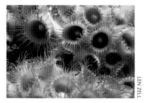

zoanthid
F. *Zoanthidea*

tube anemone
F. *Cerianthidae*

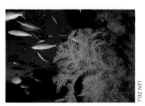

black coral
Atipathes sp.

staghorn coral
Acropora sp.

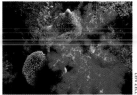

spiky soft coral
Dendronephthya sp.

lace coral
Stylaster sp.

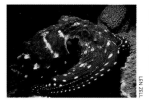

painted crayfish
Panulirus spp.

emperor shrimp
Periclemes imperator

egg cowry
Ovula ovum

octopus
Octopus sp.

giant clam
Tridacna gigas

chromodoris nudibranch
Chromodoris coi

rigid-bodied nudibranch
Notodoris gardineri

bryozoan
Ph. *Bryozoa*

feather star
Cl. *Crinoidea*

blue sea star
Linckia laevigata

sea cucumber
Thelanota anax

sea urchin
Echinometra mathaei

Hazardous Marine Life

Marine animals almost never attack divers, but many have defensive and offensive weaponry that can be triggered if they feel threatened or annoyed. The basic rule of thumb is to avoid touching all marine life. Being able to recognize potentially hazardous critters is also a good way to avoid accident or injury. The following photographs illustrate some of the GBR's most venomous and dangerous marine life, followed by short descriptions of what to expect—and recommendations for immediate first aid—in the unfortunate event you are stung, bitten or stabbed.

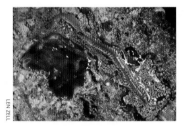

Bristle Worms

Bristle worms are errant (free-living) polychaete, or many-bristled, worms. If you touch one, its bristles can break off in your skin and cause an intense burning sensation. Use gently applied glue, tape or a facial peel to remove the fine, hair-like bristles.

Sea Jellies & Other Stingers

Sea jellies, box jellies and Portuguese man-o-wars are found in GBR waters and all have dangerous tentacles that are loaded with nematocysts (stinging cells), used to deter predators and catch prey. Upon contact, the stinging

sea jelly

cells will "fire": cut into the skin and inject venom.

Box jellies are found only along the coast. They, and the small irukandji (a type of box jelly), can deliver a fatal sting. Although caution is worthwhile, deaths by sea jellies are uncommon, and even severe stings can usually be treated with modern first

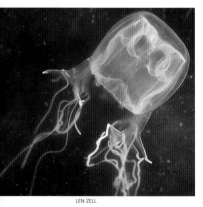

box jelly

aid. Flood sea jelly stings with a decontaminant, such as vinegar, and apply a cold compress. For others, remove any remaining tentacles with forceps or tweezers, flood the wound with ice water and maintain a cold compress.

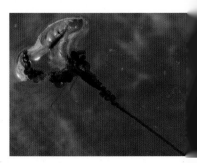

Portuguese man-o-war

Fire Coral

Fire coral appears in two basic hydro-zoan forms. Fireweed can be either white or brown and is soft, fragile and feathery. The hard form of stinging coral is either encrusting or branching and grows in yellow or brown coral colonies. The colony surface is covered in tiny hairs, each loaded with stinging cells. The hairs grow out of minute pores, giving the coral the scientific name *Millepora*. Contact results in a burning itch, which may develop into secondary infections if scratched. Irrigate with a decontaminant, such as vinegar or rubbing alcohol, and apply hydrocortisone cream.

Anemones & Corallimorpharians

corallimorpharian

Anemones and corallimorpharians use the same types of stinging cells as fire corals and sea jellies. Some anemones are totally harmless, while others can inflict painful stings and cause severe allergic reactions. Corallimorpharian stings tend to be itchier and take longer to heal. Monitor the severity of the sting, treat with a decontaminant, ice packs and local anesthetics.

Cone Shells

Cone shells are found in the shallows of most reeftops and under boulders. These attractive shells are armed with a proboscis, out of which shoots a small poisonous harpoon used to inject a highly toxic venom. In the event of a sting, the stung area will go numb. This can be followed by muscular or respiratory paralysis and even, in extreme cases, heart failure. Treat as as you would a snake bite, with a pressure bandage, and seek medical attention immediately.

Blue-Ringed Octopus

Although small—only 5 to 20cm (2 to 8 inches)—this octopus, whose blue rings flash when it's annoyed, delivers a viscious, even fatal bite. People have put shells in their wetsuits only to be surprised when a blue-ringed octopus emerges. Avoid empty shells, cans and bottles. Apply pressure bandage and seek immediate medical attention.

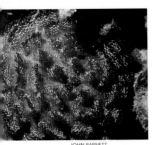

Sea Urchins & Crown-of-Thorns Sea Stars

With spines strong enough to penetrate neoprene and the skin, spiny sea urchins and crown-of-thorns sea stars (see pg. 111) are obvious creatures to avoid, especially species that have a toxic bulb at the end of the spines. Also beware the toxic pedicellariae (pincers) between the spines, which cause severe pain upon contact, and have even killed humans. Like most hazardous critters, you can completely avoid injury by not touching. Remove spine debris and soak in non-scalding hot water.

JOHN BARNETT
sea urchin

LEN ZELL

crown-of-thorns sea star

Sea Snakes

LEN ZELL

Air-breathing reptiles with a venom said to be up to 20 times stronger than any land snake, sea snakes only release venom when feeding or under extreme distress—so most defensive bites do not contain venom. If someone is bitten and injected with venom, immobilize the limb, use a pressure bandage and get help immediately. Do not wash the wound.

Stingrays

Stingrays are generally harmless and fun to watch. But be careful when walking in the shallows or kneeling on the bottom: if you accidentally tread on a ray, it will flick its tail over its head and drive the barb in its tail downward into your leg or foot. The barb can penetrate bone and can leave a venom, which is extremely painful. Remove any visible pieces of the barb or its sheath and immerse the wound in non-scalding hot water. The hot water denatures the venom and the pain is usually quick to disappear. Always shuffle your feet when walking in the shallows and check the sea floor before kneeling.

LEN ZELL

Sharks

Sharks rarely attack divers in GBR waters. Occasional bumps and rubs have caused skin abrasions or lacerations, but most sharks are relatively harmless. Incidents usually occur to people intentionally feeding sharks or carrying fish, which sharks mistake for bait. Townsville has one of the highest total shark-related death tallies in the world—but all occurred during WWII when soldiers swam in the river outlet that carried offal from the local meat works! Victims of any shark-related injury should seek immediate medical attention.

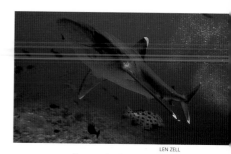

LEN ZELL

silvertip shark

LEN ZELL

Moray Eels

A moray opens and closes its mouth to breathe, which makes it look as though it's about to take a big bite. But, shy by nature, morays will generally leave you alone if you leave them alone. They will bite in unusual circumstances and when they do, they tend to hang on tight. Irrigate wounds with fresh water and antiseptics, then seek medical attention.

Barracuda

All teeth and almost no bite, barracuda often get a bad rap. Unless provoked, they rarely attack divers. They may be attracted to shiny objects—such as jewelry—that resemble fishing lures. Barracuda have sharp, backward-slanting teeth and under-slung jaws, which allow them to hang on. If you are bitten, try not to pull back quickly, to avoid nasty tears to the skin. Treat as you would a moray bite.

LEN ZELL

JOHN BARNETT

scorpionfish

Venomous Fish

Scorpionfish, stonefish, rabbitfish and lionfish are all masters of disguise with bulbs of venom at the base of their dorsal spines (or all spines in the case of the lionfish), so if you tread on one or annoy it enough, you are likely to be punctured and then injected with venom. Use non-scalding hot water to denature the venom.

LEN ZELL

Diving Conservation & Awareness

Marine Reserves & Regulations

The GBR Region is a World Heritage Area and the world's largest marine park—Australia has more reefs under its control than any other country. The areas of the GBR outside the GBRMP are in the jurisdiction of the state of Queensland or Environment Australia (Coral Sea Territories). The Torres Strait is under joint management by Australia and Papua New Guinea. Areas above low-water are in Queensland's jurisdiction and they and the GBRMP are managed by Queensland's Environmental Protection Agency (EPA).

The marine park concept is an innovative multi-use zoning system. Significant public input is used to develop marine park "zones" ranging from no-access areas to national parks (see page 42 for zone definitions). The whole area is protected from littering, oil drilling or mining. Less than 1% of the GBR is closed to recreational diving but on the entire GBR, your diving practice should follow the "look, don't touch" rule.

Whereas the GBR waters are managed by the GBRMPA, the on-site (land) management of the GBR national parks is handled by the Queensland EPA. If you wish to collect, act commercially or do anything you wouldn't do in a national park, check the rules at the nearest Marine Parks office or the GBRMPA.

Learning About the Reef

Many varieties of interpretive reef services exist on the GBR mainland, islands and boats. Probably the best mainland service is Reef Teach in Cairns. Reef Teach offers nightly slide show and a lecture given by a local marine biologist. This is an excellent way to learn about coral reef growth and reproduction, identification and reef threats, fish identification and behavior, also tips on underwater photography and diving and snorkeling on the GBR. Reef Teach is at 14 Spence St., Cairns, ☎ 4051 6882, email: learn@reefteach.com.au, website: www.reefteach.com.au. Shows start at 6:15pm daily, except Sunday.

In the water, the *Undersea Explorer* leads the way on positively linking tourism with scientific research, as they take recreational divers on research expeditions to learn more about whales, turtles, sharks, nautilus and other reef life. This live-aboard conducts its main research from Port Douglas to the outer Great

Barrier Ribbon Reefs and to Osprey Reef in the Coral Sea. In addition to a unique diving experience, you'll get to take part in valuable research while learning more about the reefs. The *Undersea Explore*r can be reached at ☎ 4099 5911, email: undersea@ozemail.com.au, website: www.undersea.com.au/subject1.html. Many other operators now take along a marine biologist or naturalist on all dive trips, to enhance divers' understanding and appreciation of the reefs.

Reefs can be successfully preserved if you look and admire but don't touch.

Government Organizations

Great Barrier Reef Marine Park Authority (GBRMPA)
Flinders St. East
P.O. Box 1379
Townsville, Qld 4810
☎ 4750 0700 fax: 4772 6093
www.gbrmpa.gov.au

Environment Australia
Manages the Coringa, Herald and Lihou National Nature Reserves in the Coral Sea

Biodiversity Group
P.O. Box 636
☎ (02) 6250 0200 fax: (02) 6250 0399
Canberra, ACT 2601

Queensland Environmental Protection Agency

Gladstone	Mackay	Townsville	Cairns
P.O. Box 5065	P.O. Box 623	P.O. Box 5391	P.O. Box 2066
Gladstone,	Mackay,	Townsville,	Cairns,
Qld 4680	Qld 4740	Qld 4810	Qld 4870
☎ 4972 6055	☎ 4951 8788	☎ 4721 2399	☎ 4052 3096
Rockhampton	**Whitsundays**	**Cardwell**	**Port Douglas**
P.O. Box 3130	P.O. Box 332	P.O. Box 74	Shop 4, Dixie St.
North Rockhampton,	Airlie Beach,	Cardwell,	Port Douglas,
Qld 4701	Qld 4802	Qld 4816	Qld 4871
☎ 4936 0511	☎ 4946 7022	☎ 4066 8601	☎ 4099 4709

Responsible Diving

Dive sites tend to be located where the reefs and walls display the most beautiful corals and sponges. It only takes a moment—an inadvertently placed hand or knee, or a careless brush or kick with a fin—to destroy this fragile, living part of our delicate ecosystem. By following certain basic guidelines while diving, you can help preserve the ecology and beauty of the reefs:

1. Never drop boat anchors onto a coral reef and take care not to ground boats on coral. Encourage dive operators and regulatory bodies in their efforts to establish permanent moorings at appropriate dive sites.

Collecting Reef Items

Collecting any item alive or dead in the GBRMP is an offense if you don't have a permit. If you want to collect anything, check with your local Marine Parks office. Permits will have various restrictions and reporting requirements. Giant clams, baler and helmet shells are fully protected. It is illegal to export any coral or shells from Australia.

2. Practice and maintain proper buoyancy control and avoid over-weighting. Be aware that buoyancy can change over the period of an extended trip. Initially you may breathe harder and need more weighting; a few days later you may breathe more easily and need less weight. Tip: Use your weight belt and tank position to maintain a horizontal position—raise them to elevate your feet, lower them to elevate your upper body. Also be careful about buoyancy loss: as you go deeper, your wetsuit compresses, as does the air in your BC.

3. Avoid touching living marine organisms with your body and equipment. Polyps can be damaged by even the gentlest contact. Never stand on or touch living coral. The use of gloves is no longer recommended: it just makes it too easy to hold on to the reef. The abrasion caused by gloves may be even more damaging to the reef than your hands are. If you must hold on to the reef, touch only exposed rock or dead coral.

4. Take great care in underwater caves. Spend as little time within them as possible, as your air bubbles can damage fragile organisms. Take turns to inspect the interior of a small cave or under a ledge to lessen the chances of damaging contact.

5. Be conscious of your fins. Even without contact, the surge from heavy fin strokes near the reef can do damage. Avoid full-leg kicks when diving close to the bottom and when leaving a photo scene. When you inadvertently kick something, stop kicking! It seems obvious, but some divers either panic or are totally oblivious when they bump something. When treading water in shallow reef areas, take care not to kick up clouds of sand. Settling sand can smother the delicate reef organisms.

6. Secure any gauges, computer consoles and octopus so they're not dangling—they are like miniature wrecking balls to a reef.

7. When swimming in strong currents, be extra careful about leg kicks and handholds.

8. Photographers should take extra precaution as cameras and equipment affect buoyancy. Changing f-stops, framing a subject and maintaining position for a photo often conspire to prohibit the ideal "no-touch" approach on a reef. When you must use "holdfasts," choose them intelligently (i.e., use one finger only for leverage off an area of dead coral).

9. Resist the temptation to collect or buy coral or shells. Aside from the ecological damage, taking home marine souvenirs depletes the beauty of a site and spoils the enjoyment of others.

10. Ensure that you take home all your trash and any litter you may find as well. Plastics in particular pose a serious threat to marine life.

11. Resist the temptation to feed fish. You may disturb their normal eating habits, encourage aggressive behavior or feed them food that is detrimental to their health.

12. Minimize your disturbance of marine animals. Don't ride on the backs of turtles or manta rays as this can cause them great anxiety.

Marine Conservation Organizations

The following groups are actively involved in promoting responsible diving practices, publicizing environmental marine threats and lobbying for better policies.

Australian Organizations

Australian Conservation Foundation
340 Gore St.
Fitzroy, Qld 3065
☎ (3) 9416 1166
fax: (3) 9416 0767
www.peg.apc.org/~acfenv

Australian Coral Reef Society
66 Oogar St.
Alexandra, Qld 4572
☎ 5443 6565
arcs@jcu.edu.au
www.tesag.jcu.edu.au/acrs

Australian Institute of Marine Science (AIMS)
PMB No. 3
Townsville MC, Qld 4810
☎ 4753 444
fax: 4772 5852
www.aims.gov.au

Australian Marine Conservation Society
P.O. Box 3139
Yeronga, Qld 4104
☎ 3848 5235
fax: 3892 5814
amcs@ozemail.com.au

Low Isles Preservation Society
Shop 4
Princes Wharf Dixie St.
Port Douglas, Qld 4871
☎ 4099 4573
fax: 4099 4849

Order of Underwater Coral Heroes (OUCH)
P.O. Box 180
Airlie Beach, Qld 4802
☎ 4946 7435
fax: 4946 5194
tfontes.@whitsunday.net.au

International Organizations

CORAL: The Coral Reef Alliance
☎ 510-848-0110
www.coral.org/

Coral Forest
☎ 415-788-REEF

www.blacktop.com/coral-forest/

Cousteau Society
☎ 757-523-9335
www.cousteau.org

Project AWARE Foundation
☎ 714-540-0251
www.projectaware.org

ReefKeeper International
☎ 305-358-4600
www.reefkeeper.org

Listings

Telephone Calls

To call Australia, dial the international access code for the country you are calling from (from the U.S. it's 011) + 61 (Australia's country code) + 7 (Queensland's area code) + the 8-digit local number. When you're in Queensland, dial 07 + the local number.

Diving Services

The following diving services are members of Dive Queensland Inc.

Bundaberg

Lady Elliot Island Holidays
P.O. Box 206, Torquay, Qld 4655
☎ 4125 5344 fax: 4125 5778
Toll-free ☎ (800) 072 200
ladyelliot@coastnet.net.au
www.coastnet.net.au/waveladyelliot
Dive Shop: yes **Instruction**: yes
Boats: 2 dive boats (7m tenders)
Trips: daytrips **Capacity**: 14

Lady Musgrave Barrier Reef Cruises
Shop 1, Bundaberg Port Marina,
Moffatt St., Bundaberg, Qld 4670
☎ 4159 4519 fax: 4159 5085
Toll-free ☎ (800) 072 110
www.ozreef.net

Dive Shop: yes **Instruction**: no
Boats: MV *Lady Musgrave* (24m, Cat 20kt),
MV *Spirit of Musgrave* (24m, Cat 23kt)
Trips: daytrips **Capacity**: 140, 70

Salty's
208 Bourbong St., Bundaberg, Qld 4670
☎ 4151 6422 fax: 4151 4938
Toll-free ☎ (800) 625 476
info@saltys.net
www.saltys.net
Dive Shop: yes **Instruction**: yes
Boats: *Lady Godiva* (7.5m, Mono 22kt)
Trips: daytrips **Capacity**: 8

Gladstone

Heron Island Resort—P&O Resorts
Heron Island, PMB, Gladstone, Qld 4680
☎ 4972 9055 fax: 4972 0244
Toll-free ☎ (800) 132 469
resorts_reservations@poaustralia.com
www.poresorts.com.au
Dive Shop: yes **Instruction**: yes
Boats: *Moray* (12m, Mono 20kt), *Noddy*
(12m, Mono 20kt), *Shearwater* (12m, Mono
20kt), *Diver* (12m, Mono 20kt), *Gatcombe*
(18m, Mono 18kt)
Trips: daytrips **Capacity**: 10-20

Capricorn Reef Diving
1/189 Musgrave St. North, Rockhampton,
Qld 4701
☎ 4922 7720 fax: 4922 7933
crd@networx.com.au
www.networx.com.au/mall/crd
Dive Shop: yes **Instruction**: yes
Boats: *Oasis* (7.5m, Mono 22kt)
Trips: daytrips **Capacity**: 10

Mackay

Mackay Adventure Divers
153 Victoria St., Mackay, Qld 4740
☎ 4953 1431 fax: 4951 1472
mad@mackay.net.au
Dive Shop: yes **Instruction**: yes
Boats: no

Elizabeth E II Coral Cruises
102 Goldsmith St., Mackay, Qld 4740
☎ 4957 4281 fax: 4957 2268
elizecc@m130.aone.net.au
Dive Shop: no **Instruction**: no
Boats: Elizabeth E II (33m, Mono 12kt)
Trips: charters **Capacity**: 28

Whitsundays

Fantasea Cruises
P.O. Box 616, Airlie Beach, Qld 4802
☎ 4946 5811 fax: 4946 5520
Toll-free ☎ (800) 650 851
fantasea@whitsunday.net.au
www.travelaustralia.cqm-au/fantasea
Dive Shop: yes **Instruction**: yes
Boats: MV *Fantasea 1* (30m, Cat 26kt)
Trips: daytrips, overnight on pontoon
Capacity: 400, 8 on overnight pontoon

H2O Sportz Hamilton Island
P.O. Box 19, Hamilton Island, Qld 4803
☎ 4946 9888 fax: 4946 9888
www.h2osportz.com.au
Dive Shop: yes **Instruction**: yes
Boats: *Reef Tripper* (16m, Cat 20kt)
Trips: daytrips **Capacity**: 30

Kelly Dive
P.O. Box 1025, Airlie Beach, Qld 4802
☎ 4946 6122 fax: 4946 4368
Toll-free ☎ (800) 063 454
kelly@whitsunday.net.au
www.kellydive.com.au
Dive Shop: yes **Instruction**: yes
Boats: MV *Swordfish* (20m, Mono 11kt),
Anaconda III (30m, MaxiYt 12kt)
Trips: 3-day trips **Capacity**: 19, 28

Oceania Dive
P.O. Box 1060, Airlie Beach, Qld 4802
☎ 4946 6032 fax: 4946 6032
Toll-free ☎ (800) 075 035
oceania@whitsunday.net.au
Dive Shop: yes **Instruction**: yes
Boats: *Oceania* (27m, Cat 25kt)
Trips: 3-day trips **Capacity**: 28

Reef Dive
Shute Harbour Rd., Airlie Beach, Qld 4802
☎ 4946 6508 fax: 4946 5007
reefdive@whitsunday.net.au
reefdive.com.au
Dive Shop: yes **Instruction**: yes
Boats: *Romance* (22m, Mot/Sail 10kt),
Tropic Princess (24m, Cat 10kt)
Prodiver (Mono 22kt)
Trips: 3-day trips **Capacity**: 18, 26, 30

Whitsunday Diver
P.O. Box 481, Airlie Beach, Qld 4802
☎ 4946 5366 fax: 4946 6033
reefbook@whitsundaydiver.com.au
www.whitsundaydiver.com.au
Dive Shop: no **Instruction**: no
Boats: *Reefjet* (23m, Mono 28kt)
Trips: daytrips **Capacity**: 68

Townsville

Coral Princess Cruises
Level 1, Suite 2 Breakwater Terminal,
Townsville, Qld 4810
☎ 4721 1673 fax: 4721 1335
Toll-free ☎ (800) 079 545
cruisecp@coralprincess.com.au
www.coralprincess.com.au
Dive Shop: no **Instruction**: no
Boats: *Coral Princess* (35m, Cat 10kt),
Coral Princess II (35m, Cat 10kt)
Trips: 3-day trips **Capacity**: 54, 50

Magnetic Island Dive Centre
P.O. Box 75, Magnetic Island, Qld 4819
☎ 4758 1399 fax: 4778 5222
trimix@ultra.net.au
Dive Shop: yes **Instruction**: yes
Boats: *Kevin* (6m, inflatable 18kt)
Trips: daytrips **Capacity**: 10

Mike Ball Dive Expeditions
252 Walker St., Townsville, Qld 4810
☎ 4772 3022 fax: 4721 2152
Toll-free ☎ (800) 643 216
resv@mikeball.com.au
www.mikeball.com
Dive Shop: yes **Instruction**: yes
Boats: *Supersport* (30m, Cat 15kt),
Spoilsport (33m, Cat 15kt),
Watersport (26m, Cat 8kt)
Trips: 3-day trips **Capacity**: 26 each boat

The Dive Bell
16 Dean St. South, Townsville, Qld 4810
☎ 4721 1155 fax: 4772 3119
enq@divebell.com
www.divebell.com
Dive Shop: yes **Instruction**: yes
Boats: *Hero* (20m, Mono 10kt)
Trips: 2- to 5-day trips **Capacity**: 14

Cairns

Cairns Dive Centre
P.O. Box 2401, Cairns, Qld 4870
☎ 4051 0294 fax: 4051 7531
Toll-free ☎ (800) 642 591
info@cairnsdive.com.au
www.cairnsdive.com.au
Dive Shop: yes **Instruction**: yes
Boats: *Coral Reeftel* (30m, Cat 8kt, permanent on reefs), *Sunkist* (20m, Mono 20kt)
Trips: overnight on *Coral Reeftel*; daytrips
Capacity: 38, 50

Captain Cook Cruises
P.O. Box 4927, Cairns, Qld 4870
☎ 4031 4433 fax: 4031 6983
Toll-free ☎ (800) 221 080
ccbreef@internetnorth.com.au
www.captcookcrus.com.au
Dive Shop: no **Instruction**: no
Boats: *Reef Endeavour* (73m, Mono 8kt)
Trips: 3- or 4-day trips **Capacity**: 150

Deep Sea Divers Den
P.O. Box 5264, Cairns, Qld 4870
☎ 4031 2223 fax: 4031 1210
info@divers-den.com
www.divers-den.com
Dive Shop: yes **Instruction**: yes
Boats: *Ocean Quest* (28m, Cat 8kt, permanent on reefs), *SeaQuest* (20m Mono 18kt),
ReefQuest (19m, Mono 18kt)
Trips: overnight on *Ocean Quest*; daytrips
Capacity: 40, 35, 40

Dive 7 Seas/Cairns Dive Academy
129 Abbot St., Cairns, Qld 4870
☎ 4041 2700 fax: 4041 2711
Dive Shop: yes **Instruction**: yes
Boats: *Outer Edge* (20m, Mono 18kt)
Trips: daytrips **Capacity**: 26

Down Under Dive
155 Sheridan St., Cairns, Qld 4870
☎ 4031 1288 fax: 4031 1373
Toll-free ☎ (800) 079 099
dudive@ozemail.com.au
www.ozemail.com.au/~dudive
Dive Shop: yes **Instruction**: yes
Boats: *Atlantic Clipper* (40m, Tallship 8kt, permanent on reefs), *Scuba Roo* (17m, Mono 18kt), *Super Cat* (18.5m, Cat 18kt)
Trips: overnight on *Atlantic Clipper*; daytrips
Capacity: 44, 50, 100

Great Diving Adventures
P.O. Box 898, Cairns, Qld 4870
☎ 4051 5644 fax: 4031 3648
Toll-free ☎ (800) 079 080
dive@greatadventures.com.au
www.greatadventures.com.au
Dive Shop: yes **Instruction**: yes
Boats: *Dive II* (11m, Cat 10kt) *PT Diver II* (10m, Mono 15kt, tender), *Tinduck 2* (7m, tender), *Reefrider* (10m, Cat 12kt, tender)
Trips: daytrips **Capacity**: 20, 23, 15, 26

Hostel Reef Trips
P.O. Box 2488, Cairns, Qld 4870
☎ 4031 7217 fax: 4031 7217
Toll-free ☎ (800) 815 811
reeftrip@cairns.net.au
www.reeftrip.com
Dive Shop: no **Instruction**: yes
Boats: *Reef Encounter* (33m, Mono 12k, permanent on reefs), *Compass* (33m, Mono 12kt)
Trips: overnight on *Reef Encounter*; daytrips
Capacity: 28, 116

Cairns (continued)

Mike Ball Dive Expeditions-Cairns
28 Spence St., Cairns, Qld 4870
☎ 4031 5484 fax: 4031 5470
Toll-free ☎ (800) 643 216
resv@mikeball.com.au
www.mikeball.com
Dive Shop: yes **Instruction**: yes
See Mike Ball—Townsville listing for boat details

Nimrod III Dive Adventures
46 Spence St., Cairns, Qld 4870
☎ 4031 5566 fax: 4031 2431
nimrod@internetnorth.com.au
internetnorth.com.au/nimrod/
Dive Shop: no **Instruction**: no
Boats: *Nimrod III* (20m, Cat 8kt)
Trips: 3-day trips **Capacity**: 18

Ocean Free
8 Bradford St., Whitfield, Cairns Qld 4870
☎ 4053 6841 fax: 40536841
oceanfree@internetnorth.com.au
Boats: 64' sailing schooner
Trips: daytrips **Capacity**: 35

Ocean Spirit Cruises
P.O. Box 2140, Cairns, Qld 4870
☎ 4031 2920 fax: 4031 4344
Toll-free ☎ (800) 644 227
ospirit@internetnorth.com.au
www.oceanspirit.com.au
Dive Shop: no **Instruction**: no
Boats: *Ocean Spirit 1* (25m, Sailcat 12kt), *Ocean Spirit II* (25m, Sailcat 12kt)
Trips: daytrips **Capacity**: 150, 100

Passions of Paradise
P.O. Box 2145, Cairns, Qld 4870
☎ 4041 1600 fax: 4051 9505
passions@iig.com.au
www.passionsofparadise.com
Dive Shop: no **Instruction**: no
Boats: *Passions of Paradise* (20m, Sailcat 9kt)
Trips: daytrips **Capacity**: 60

Pro Dive Cairns
P.O. Box 5551, Cairns, Qld 4870
☎ 4031 5255 fax: 4051 9955
Toll-free ☎ (800) 353 213
prodive@internetnorth.com.au
www.prodive-cairns.com.au

Dive Shop: yes **Instruction**: yes
Boats: *Scuba Pro* (24m, Mono 15kt), *Kalinda* (21m, Mono 10kt)
Trips: 3-day trips **Capacity**: 32, 25

Quintessential Diving
P.O. Box 157N, Cairns, Qld 4870
☎ 4038 2304 fax: 4038 2304
Dive Shop: no **Instruction**: no
Boats: *Falla* (22m, Lugger 8kt)
Trips: daytrips **Capacity**: 30

Reef Magic Cruises
P.O. Box 905, Cairns, Qld 4870
☎ 4031 1588 fax: 4031 3318
reef.magic@altnews.com.au
www.reefmagic.com.au
Dive Shop: yes **Instruction**: yes
Boats: *Reef Magic* (22m, Cat 21kt)
Trips: daytrips **Capacity**: 145

Rum Runner Dive Adventures
P.O. Box 6608, Cairns, Qld 4870
☎ 4050 9988 fax: 4050 9911
Toll-free ☎ (800) 803 103
sales@rumrunner.com.au
www.rumrunner.com.au/rumrunner/
Dive Shop: yes **Instruction**: no
Boats: *Rum Runner I* (20m, Mot/Sail 9kt), *Rum Runner III* (20m, Mono 9kt)
Trips: 4-day trips **Capacity**: 16, 18

Santa Maria Yacht Cruises
P.O. Box 5957, Cairns, Qld 4870
☎ 4031 0558 fax: 4051 5278
smaria@ozemail.com.au
www.ozemail.com.au/~smaria/
Dive Shop: no **Instruction**: no
Boats: *Santa Maria* (20m, Schooner 9kt)
Trips: 3-day trips **Capacity**: 10

Sunlover Cruises
P.O. Box 835, Cairns, Qld 4870
☎ 4035 2444 fax: 4035 2253
Toll-free ☎ (800) 810 512
res@sunlover.com.au
www.sunlover.com.au
Dive Shop: no **Instruction**: no
Boats: *Tropic Sunseeker* (34m, Cat 22kt), *Tropic Sunbird* (33m, Cat 22kt)
Trips: daytrips **Capacity**: 300 each boat

Taka II Dive Adventures
131 Lake St., Cairns, Qld 4870
☎ 4051 8722 fax: 4031 2739
takadive@ozemail.com.au
www.taka.com.au
Dive Shop: yes **Instruction**: no
Boats: *Taka II* (22m, Mono 11kt)
Trips: 5-day trips **Capacity**: 26

TUSA Dive Charters
P.O. Box 1276, Cairns, Qld 4870
☎ 4031 1248 fax: 4031 5221
tusa@c130.aone.net.au
www.tusadive.com
Dive Shop: yes **Instruction**: yes
Boats: *TUSA III* (21m, Mono 20kt), *Tusa IV* (22m, Mono 20kt)
Trips: daytrips; *Tusa IV* charters **Capacity**: 27

Port Douglas

Poseidon Outer Reef Cruises
P.O. Box 431, Port Douglas, Qld 4871
☎ 4099 4772 fax: 4099 4134
poseidon@internetnorth.com.au
www.poseidon-cruises.com.au
Dive Shop: yes **Instruction**: yes
Boats: *Poseidon* (20m, Cat 22kt)
Trips: daytrips **Capacity**: 48

Quicksilver Dive Services
P.O. Box 228, Port Douglas, Qld 4871
☎ 4099 5050 fax: 4099 4065
dive@quicksilverdive.com.au
www.quicksilverdive.com.au
Dive Shop: yes **Instruction**: yes

Boats: *Quicksilver Connection I* (46m, Cat 33kt), *Quicksilver Connection II* (39m, Cat 33kt), *Wave Dancer* (30m, Sailcat 12kt), *Diversity* (28m, Cat 18kt), *Nemomono* (16m, Mono 17kt)
Trips: daytrips; charters **Capacity**: 440, 300, 156, 30, 24

Undersea Explorer
P.O. Box 615, Port Douglas, Qld 4871
☎ 4099 5911 fax: 4099 5914
Toll-free ☎ (800) 648 877
undersea@ozemail.com.au
www.undersea.com.au
Dive Shop: no **Instruction**: no
Boats: *Undersea Explorer* (25m, Mono 9kt)
Trips: 6-day trips **Capacity**: 19+3 scientists

Cape Tribulation

Rum Runner Cape Tribulation
P.O. Box 6608, Cairns, Qld 4870
☎ 4050 9988 fax: 4050 9911
Toll-free ☎ (800) 803 103
sales@rumrunner.com.au

www.rumrunner.com.au/rumrunner/
Dive Shop: no **Instruction**: yes
Boats: *Rum Runner IX* (16m, Sailcat 12kt)
Trips: daytrips **Capacity**: 45

Bloomfield River

Big Mama
Bloodwood Rd., Bloomfield River, Cooktown, Qld 4871
☎ 4060 8011 fax: 4060 8234
sail@bigmama.com.au

www.bigmama.com.au
Dive Shop: no **Instruction**: no
Boats: *Big Mama* (18m, Mot/Sail 9kt)
Trips: daytrips/charters **Capacity**: 12

Equipment Repairs

Cairns Scuba Air
P.O. Box 1380, Cairns, Qld 4870
☎ 4035 5035 fax: 4035 5387
scuba.air@iig.com.au

Scuba Quip
15 Amaroo Close, Smithfield Hts.,
Cairns, Qld 4878
☎ 4038 1569 fax: 4038 1569

Dive Travel Agents

Diversion Dive Travel
P.O. Box 715, Smithfield, Cairns, Qld 4878
☎ 4039 0200 fax: 4039 0300
info@diversionOZ.com.au
www.diversionOZ.com

The Adventure Company Australia
P.O. Box 5740, Cairns, Qld 4870
☎ 4051 4777 fax: 4051 4888
adventures@adventures.com.au
www.adventures.com.au

Local Tourist Offices

Bundaberg
Corner of Takalvan & Bourbong Sts.
☎ 4172 2406

Gladstone
100 Goondoon St.
☎ 4972 4000

Mackay
Nebo Rd., south of city center
☎ 4952 2677

Airlie Beach
348 Shute Harbour Rd.
☎ 4946 6673

Townsville
Pacific Highway south of city
☎ 4778 3555 (main office) or
☎ 4721 3660 (city mall booth)

Port Douglas
27 Macrossan St.
☎ 4099 5599

Cairns
There are numerous privately run information centers, which act as booking agents. The **Wet Tropics Information Centre** on Esplanade across from the Shields St. corner combines information with displays on the far north rainforest and reef environments. Local phone books have listings of all the individual information centers.

Index

dive sites covered in this book appear in **bold** type

Lonely Planet Pisces Books

The **Diving & Snorkeling** guides cover top destinations worldwide. Beautifully illustrated with full-color photos throughout, the series explores the best diving and snorkeling areas and prepares divers for what to expect when they get there. Each site is described in detail, with information on suggested ability levels, depth, visibility and, of course, marine life. There's basic topside information as well for each destination.

Also check out dive guides to:

Australia: Southeast Coast

Bahamas: Family Islands & Grand Bahama

Bahamas: Nassau & New Providence

Bali & the Komodo Region

British Virgin Islands

Cayman Islands

Cocos Island

Curaçao

Dominica

Fiji

Florida Keys

Jamaica

Northern California & Monterey Peninsula

Pacific Northwest

Palau

Puerto Rico

Red Sea

Roatan & Honduras' Bay Islands

Scotland

Seychelles

Southern California

St. Maarten, Saba, & St. Eustatius

Texas

Truk Lagoon

Turks & Caicos

U.S. Virgin Islands

Vanuatu

Lonely Planet Series Descriptions

Lonely Planet **travel guides** explore a destination in depth with options to suit a range of budgets. With reliable, practical advice on getting around, restaurants and accommodations, these easy-to-use guides also include detailed maps, color photographs, extensive background material and coverage of sites both on and off the beaten track.

For budget travelers **shoestring guides** are the best single source of travel information covering an entire continent or large region. Written by experienced travelers these 'tried and true' classics offer reliable, first-hand advice on transportation, restaurants and accommodations, and insider tips for avoiding bureaucratic confusion and stretching money as far as possible.

City guides cover many of the world's great cities with full-color photographs throughout, front and back cover gatefold maps, and information for every traveler's budget and style. With information for business travelers, all the best places to eat and shop and itinerary suggestions for long and short-term visitors, city guides are a complete package.

Lonely Planet **phrasebooks** have essential words and phrases to help travelers communicate with the locals. With color tabs for quick reference, an extensive vocabulary, use of local scripts and easy-to-follow pronunciation instructions, these handy, pocket-sized language guides cover most situations a traveler is likely to encounter.

Lonely Planet **walking guides** cover some of the world's most exciting trails. With detailed route descriptions including degrees of difficulty and best times to go, reliable maps and extensive background information, these guides are an invaluable resource for both independent hikers and those in organized groups.

Lonely Planet **travel atlases** are thoroughly researched and fact-checked by the guidebook authors to ensure they complement the books. The handy format means none of the holes, wrinkles, tears or constant folding and refolding of flat maps. They include background information in five languages.

Journeys is a new series of travel literature that captures the spirit of a place, illuminates a culture, recounts an adventure and introduces a fascinating way of life. Written by a diverse group of writers, they are tales to read while on the road or at home in your favorite armchair.

Entertaining, independent and adventurous, Lonely Planet **videos** encourage the same approach to travel as the guidebooks. Currently broadcast throughout the world, this award-winning series features all original footage and music.

Where to Find Us . . .

Lonely Planet is known worldwide for publishing practical, reliable and no-nonsense travel information in our guides and on our website. The Lonely Planet list covers just about every accessible part of the world. Currently there are nine series: *Pisces books, travel guides, shoestring guides, walking guides, city guides, phrasebooks, audio packs, travel atlases* and *Journeys*–a unique collection of travel writing.

Lonely Planet Publications

Australia
P.O. Box 617, Hawthorn 3122, Victoria
☎ (03) 9819 1877 fax: (03) 9819 6459
email: talk2us@lonelyplanet.com.au

USA
150 Linden Street
Oakland, California 94607
☎ (510) 893 8555, (800) 275 8555
fax: (510) 893 8563
email: info@lonelyplanet.com

UK
10A Spring Place,
London NW5 3BH
☎ (0171) 428 4800 fax: (0171) 428 4828
email: go@lonelyplanet.co.uk

France
1 rue du Dahomey
75011 Paris
☎ 01 55 25 33 00 fax: 01 55 25 33 01
email: bip@lonelyplanet.fr

www.lonelyplanet.com